The Possibilities of Prayer

The Possibilities of Prayer

Annotated

E. M. Bounds

Waymark Books

Copyright © 2023 by Waymark Books

This is a proofread and newly designed edition of a public domain work.

CONTENTS

1. The Ministry of Prayer — 1
2. Prayer and the Promises — 4
3. Prayer and the Promises (Continued) — 10
4. Prayer—It's Possibilities — 17
5. Prayer—It's Possibilities (Continued) — 25
6. Prayer—It's Possibilities (Continued) — 30
7. Prayer—It's Wide Range — 35
8. Prayer—Facts and History — 40
9. Prayer—Facts and History (Continued) — 46
10. Answered Prayer — 51
11. Answered Prayer (Continued) — 58
12. Answered Prayer (Continued) — 63
13. Prayer Miracles — 69

CONTENTS

14 Wonders of God Through Prayer — 77

15 Prayer and Divine Providence — 88

16 Prayer and Divine Providence (Continued) — 97

APPENDIX: E. M. BOUNDS AND THE BOOKS HE WROTE — 103

1

The Ministry of Prayer

THE ministry of prayer has been the peculiar distinction of all of God's saints. This has been the secret of their power. The energy and the soul of their work has been the closet. The need of help outside of man being so great, man's natural inability to always judge kindly, justly, and truly, and to act the Golden Rule, so prayer is enjoined by Christ to enable man to act in all these things according to the divine will. By prayer, the ability is secured to feel the law of love, to speak according to the law of love, and to do everything in harmony with the law of love.

God can help us. God is a father. We need God's good things to help us to "do justly, to love mercy, and to walk humbly before God." We need divine aid to act brotherly, wisely, and nobly, and to judge truly, and charitably. God's help to do all these things in God's way is secured by prayer. "Ask, and ye shall receive; seek, and ye shall find; knock, and it shall be opened unto you."

In the marvelous output of Christian graces and duties, the result of giving ourselves wholly to God, recorded in the twelfth chapter of Romans, we have the words, "Continuing instant in prayer," preceded by "rejoicing in hope, patient in tribulation," followed by, "Distributing to the necessity of the saints, given to hospitality." Paul thus writes as if these rich and rare graces and unselfish duties, so sweet, bright, generous, and unselfish, had for their center and source the ability to pray.

This is the same word which is used of the prayer of the disciples which ushered in Pentecost with all of its rich and glorious blessings of the Holy Spirit. In Colossians, Paul presses the word into the service of prayer again, "Continue in prayer, and watch in the same with thanksgiving." The word in its background and root means strong, the ability to stay, and persevere steadfast, to hold fast and firm, to give constant attention to.

In Acts, chapter six, it is translated, "Give ourselves continually to prayer." There is in it constancy, courage, unfainting perseverance. It means giving such marked attention to, and such deep concern to a thing, as will make it conspicuous and controlling.

This is an advance in demand on "continue." Prayer is to be incessant, without intermission, earnestly, no check in desire, in spirit or in act, the spirit and the life always in the attitude of prayer. The knees may not always be bent, the lips may not always be vocal with words of prayer, but the spirit is always in the act of prayer.

There ought to be no adjustment of life or spirit for closet hours. The closet spirit should sweetly rule and adjust all times and occasions. Our activities and work should be performed in the same spirit which makes our devotion and closet time sacred. "Without intermission, incessantly, earnestly," describes an opulence, and energy, and unabated and ceaseless strength and fullness of effort; like the full and exhaustless and spontaneous flow of an artesian stream. Touch the man of God who thus understands prayer, at any point, at any time, and a full current of prayer is seen flowing from him.

But all these untold benefits, of which the Holy Spirit is made to us the conveyor, go back in their disposition and results to prayer. Not on a little process and a mere performance of prayer is the coming of the Holy Spirit and of his great grace conditioned, but on prayer set on fire, by an unquenchable desire, with such a sense of need as cannot be denied, with a fixed determination which will not let go, and which will never faint till it wins the greatest good and gets the best and last blessing God has in store for us.

The first Christ, Jesus, our great high priest, forever blessed and adored be his name, was a gracious comforter, a faithful guide, a gifted teacher, a fearless advocate, a devoted friend, and an all-powerful intercessor. The other, "another comforter," the Holy Spirit, comes into all these blessed relations of fellowship, authority and aid, with all the tenderness, sweetness, fulness and efficiency of the first Christ.

Was the first Christ, the Christ of prayer? Did he offer prayers and supplications, with strong crying and tears unto God? Did he seek the silence, the solitude and the darkness that he might pray unheard and unwitnessed save by heaven, in his wrestling agony, for man with God? Does he ever live, enthroned above at the Father's right hand, there to pray for us?

Then how truly does the other Christ, the other comforter, the Holy Spirit, represent Jesus Christ as the Christ of prayer! This other Christ, the comforter, plants himself not in the waste of the mountain nor far into the night, but in the chill and the night of the human heart, to rouse it to the struggle, and to teach it the need and form of prayer. How the divine comforter, the spirit of truth, puts into the human heart the burden of earth's almighty need, and makes the human lips give voice to its mute and unutterable groanings!

What a mighty Christ of prayer is the Holy Spirit! How he quenches every flame in the heart but the flame of heavenly desire! How he quiets, like a weaned child, all the self-will, until in will, in brain, and in heart, and by mouth, we pray only as he prays. "Making intercession for the saints, according to the will of God."

2

Prayer and the Promises

WITHOUT the promise prayer is eccentric and baseless. Without prayer, the promise is dim, voiceless, shadowy, and impersonal. The promise makes prayer dauntless and irresistible. The apostle Peter declares that God has given to us "exceeding great and precious promises." "Precious" and "exceeding great" promises they are, and for this very cause we are to "add to our faith," and supply virtue. It is the addition which makes the promises current and beneficial to us. It is prayer which makes the promises weighty, precious and practical. The apostle Paul did not hesitate to declare that God's grace so richly promised was made operative and efficient by prayer. "Ye also helping together by prayer for us."

The promises of God are "exceeding great and precious," words which clearly indicate their great value and their broad reach, as grounds upon which to base our expectations in praying. Howsoever exceeding great and precious they are, their realization, the possibility and condition of that realization, are based on prayer. How glorious are these promises to the believing saints and to the whole church! How the brightness and bloom, the fruitage and cloudless midday glory of the future beam on us through the promises of God! Yet these promises never brought hope to bloom or fruit to a prayerless heart. Neither could these promises, were they a thousandfold increased in number and preciousness, bring millennium glory to a prayerless church. Prayer makes the promise rich, fruitful and a conscious reality.

Prayer as a spiritual energy, and illustrated in its enlarged and mighty working, makes way for and brings into practical realization the promises of God.

God's promises cover all things which pertain to life and godliness, which relate to body and soul, which have to do with time and eternity. These promises bless the present and stretch out in their benefactions to the illimitable and eternal future. Prayer holds these promises in keeping and in fruition. Promises are God's golden fruit to be plucked by the hand of prayer. Promises are God's incorruptible seed, to be sown and tilled by prayer.

Prayer and the promises are interdependent. The promise inspires and energizes prayer, but prayer locates the promise, and gives it realization and location. The promise is like the blessed rain falling in full showers, but prayer, like the pipes which transmit, preserve and direct the rain, localizes and precipitates these promises, until they become local and personal, and bless, refresh and fertilize. Prayer takes hold of the promise and conducts it to its marvelous ends, removes the obstacles, and makes a highway for the promise to its glorious fulfillment.

While God's promises are "exceeding great and precious," they are specific, clear and personal. How pointed and plain God's promise to Abraham:

And the angel of the Lord called unto Abraham out of heaven the second time, And said, "By myself have I sworn, saith the Lord, for because thou hast done this thing, and hast not withheld thy son, thine only son; That in blessing I will bless thee, and in multiplying I will multiply thy seed as the stars of heaven, and as the sand which is upon the seashore; and thy seed shall possess the gate of his enemies; And in thy seed shall all the nations of the earth be blessed; because thou hast obeyed my voice."

But Rebekah through whom the promise is to flow is childless. Her barren womb forms an invincible obstacle to the fulfillment of God's promise. But in the course of time children are born to her.

Isaac becomes a man of prayer through whom the promise is to be realized, and so we read:

"And Isaac entreated the Lord for his wife, because she was barren, and the Lord was entreated for him, and Rebekah his wife conceived."

Isaac's praying opened the way for the fulfillment of God's promise, and carried it on to its marvelous fulfillment, and made the promise effectual in bringing forth marvelous results.

God spoke to Jacob and made definite promises to him:

"Return unto the land of thy fathers, and to thy kindred, and I will be with thee."

Jacob promptly moves out on the promise, but Esau confronts him with his awakened vengeance and his murderous intention, more dreadful because of the long years, unappeased and waiting. Jacob throws himself directly on God's promise by a night of prayer, first in quietude and calmness, and then when the stillness, the loneliness and the darkness of the night are upon him, he makes the all-night wrestling prayer.

> With thee I mean all night to stay,
> And wrestle till the break of day.

God's being is involved, his promise is at stake, and much is involved in the issue. Esau's temper, his conduct and his character are involved. It is a notable occasion. Much depends upon it. Jacob pursues his case and presses his plea with great struggles and hard wrestling. It is the highest form of importunity. But the victory is gained at last. His name and nature are changed and he becomes a new and different man. Jacob himself is saved first of all. He is blessed in his life and soul. But more still is accomplished. Esau undergoes a radical change of mind. He who came forth with hate and revenge in his heart against his own brother, seeking Jacob's destruction, is strangely and wonderfully affected, and

THE POSSIBILITIES OF PRAYER

he is changed and his whole attitude toward his brother becomes radically different. And when the two brothers meet, love takes the place of fear and hate, and they vie with each other in showing true brotherly affection.

The promise of God is fulfilled. But it took all that night of importunate praying to do the deed. It took that fearful night of wrestling on Jacob's part to make the promise sure and cause it to bear fruit. Prayer wrought the marvelous deed. So prayer of the same kind will produce like results in this day. It was God's promise and Jacob's praying which crowned and crowded the results so wondrously.

"Go show thyself to Ahab and I will send rain on the earth," was God's command and promise to his servant Elijah after the sore famine had cursed the land. Many glorious results marked that day of heroic faith and dauntless courage on Elijah's part. The sublime issue with Israel had been successful, the fire had fallen, Israel had been reclaimed, the prophets of Baal had been killed, but there was no rain. The one thing, the only thing, which God had promised, had not been given. The day was declining, and the awestruck crowds were faint, and yet held by an invisible hand.

Elijah turns from Israel to God and from Baal to the one source of help for a final issue and a final victory. But seven times is the restless eagerness of the prophet stayed. Not till the seventh repeated time is his vigilance rewarded and the promise pressed to its final fulfillment. Elijah's fiery, relentless praying bore to its triumphant results the promise of God, and rain descended in full showers.

> Thy promise, Lord, is ever sure,
> And they that in thy house would dwell
> That happy station to secure,
> Must still in holiness excel.

Our prayers are too little and feeble to execute the purposes or to claim the promises of God with appropriating power. Marvelous purposes need marvelous praying to execute them. Miracle-making promises need miraclemaking praying to realize them. Only divine praying can operate divine promises or carry out divine purposes. How great, how sublime, and how exalted are the promises God makes to his people! How eternal are the purposes of God! Why are we so impoverished in experience and so low in life when God's promises are so "exceeding great and precious"? Why do the eternal purposes of God move so tardily? Why are they so poorly executed? Our failure to appropriate the divine promises and rest our faith on them, and to pray believingly is the solution. "We have not because we ask not." We ask and receive not because we ask amiss.

Prayer is based on the purpose and promise of God. Prayer is submission to God. Prayer has no sigh of disloyalty against God's will. It may cry out against the bitterness and the dread weight of an hour of unutterable anguish: "If it be possible, let this cup pass from me." But it is surcharged with the sweetest and promptest submission. "Yet not my will, but thine be done."

But prayer in its usual uniform and deep current is conscious conformity to God's will, based upon the direct promise of God's Word, and under the illumination and application of the Holy Spirit. Nothing is surer than that the Word of God is the sure foundation of prayer. We pray just as we believe God's Word. Prayer is based directly and specifically upon God's revealed promises in Christ Jesus. It has no other ground upon which to base its plea. All else is shadowy, sandy, fickle. Not our feelings, not our merits, not our works, but God's promise is the basis of faith and the solid ground of prayer.

> Now I have found the ground wherein
> Sure my soul's anchor may remain;
> The wounds of Jesus-for my sin,
> Before the world's foundation slain.

The converse of this proposition is also true. God's promises are dependent and conditioned upon prayer to appropriate them and make them a conscious realization. The promises are inwrought in us, appropriated by us, and held in the arms of faith by prayer. Let it be noted that prayer gives the promises their efficiency, localizes and appropriates them, and utilizes them. Prayer puts the promises to practical and present uses. Prayer puts the promises as the seed in the fructifying soil. Promises, like the rain are general. Prayer embodies, precipitates, and locates them for personal use. Prayer goes by faith into the great fruit orchard of God's exceeding great and precious promises, and with hand and heart picks the ripest and richest fruit. The promises, like electricity, may sparkle and dazzle and yet be impotent for good till these dynamic, life-giving currents are chained by prayer, and are made the mighty forces which move and bless.

3

Prayer and the Promises (Continued)

THE great promises find their fulfillment along the lines of prayer. They inspire prayer, and through prayer the promises flow out to their full realization and bear their ripest fruit.

The magnificent and sanctifying promise in Ezekiel, thirty-sixth chapter, a promise finding its full, ripe, and richest fruit in the New Testament, is an illustration of how the promise waits on prayer:

Then will I sprinkle clean water upon you, and ye shall be clean; from all your filthiness, and from all your idols will I cleanse you. A new heart also will I give you, and a new spirit will I put within you; and I will take away the stony heart out of your flesh, and I will give you a heart of flesh. And I will put my Spirit within you, and cause you to walk in my statutes, and ye shall keep my judgments and do them. And ye shall dwell in the land that I gave to your fathers; and ye shall be my people, and I will be your God.

And concerning this promise, and this work, God definitely says:

"I will yet for this be inquired of by the house of Israel, to do it for them."

The more truly men have prayed for these rich things, the more fully have they entered into this exceeding great and precious promise, for in its initial, and final results as well as in all of its processes, realized, it is entirely dependent on prayer.

> Give me a new, a perfect heart,
> From doubt, and fear, and sorrow free;
> The mind which was in Christ impart,
> And let my spirit cleave to thee.
> "0 take this heart of stone away!
> Thy sway it doth not, cannot own;
> In me no longer let it stay;
> 0 take away this heart of stone!"

No new heart ever throbbed with its pulsations of divine life in one whose lips have never sought in prayer with contrite spirit, that precious boon of a perfect heart of love and cleanness. God never has put his Spirit into the realm of a human heart which had never invoked by ardent praying the coming and indwelling of the Holy Spirit. A prayerless spirit has no affinity for a clean heart. Prayer and a pure heart go hand in hand. Purity of heart follows praying, while prayer is the natural, spontaneous outflowing of a heart made clean by the blood of Jesus Christ.

In this connection let it be noted that God's promises are always personal and specific. They are not general, indefinite, vague. They do not have to do with multitudes and classes of people in a mass, but are directed to individuals. They deal with persons. Each believer can claim the promise as his own. God deals with each one personally. So that every saint can put the promises to the test. "Prove me now herewith, saith the Lord." No need of generalizing, nor of being lost in vagueness. The praying saint has the right to put his hand upon the promise and claim it as his own, one made especially to him, and one intended to embrace all his needs, present and future.

> Though troubles assail,
> And dangers affright,
> Though friends should all fail,
> And foes all unite,
> Yet one thing secures us,
> Whatever betide,
> The promise assures us,
> The Lord will provide.

Jeremiah once said, speaking of the captivity of Israel and of its ending, speaking for Almighty God: "After seventy years be accomplished at Babylon, I will visit you, and will perform my good word toward you, in causing you to return to this place."

But this strong and definite promise of God was accompanied by these words, coupling the promise with prayer: "Then shall ye call upon me, and ye shall go and pray unto me, and I will hearken unto you. And ye shall seek me and find me, when ye shall search for me with all your heart." This seems to indicate very clearly that the promise was dependent for its fulfillment on prayer.

In Daniel we have this record,

"I, Daniel, understood by books the number of the years whereof the word of the Lord came to Jeremiah, the prophet, that he would accomplish seventy years in the desolations of Jerusalem. And I set my face unto the Lord God to seek by prayer and supplications with fastings and sackcloth and ashes."

So Daniel, as the time of the captivity was expiring, set himself in mighty prayer in order that the promise should be fulfilled and the captivity be brought to an end. It was God's promise by Jeremiah and Daniel's praying which broke the chains of Babylonian captivity, set Israel free and brought God's ancient people back to their native land. The promise and prayer went together to carry out God's purpose and to execute his plans.

THE POSSIBILITIES OF PRAYER

God had promised through his prophets that the coming Messiah should have a forerunner. How many homes and wombs in Israel had longed for the coming to them of this great honor! Perchance Zachariah and Elizabeth were the only ones who were trying to realize by prayer this great dignity and blessing. At least we do know that the angel said to Zachariah, as he announced to him the coming of this great personage, "Thy prayer is heard." It was then that the word of the Lord as spoken by the prophets and the prayer of the old priest and his wife brought John the Baptist into the withered womb, and into the childless home of Zachariah and Elizabeth.

The promise given to Paul, engraven on his apostolic commission, as related by him after his arrest in Jerusalem, when he was making his defense before King Agrippa, was on this wise: "Delivering thee from the people and from the Gentiles, unto whom I now send thee." How did Paul make this promise efficient? How did he make the promise real? Here is the answer. In trouble by men, Jew and Gentile, pressed by them sorely, he writes to his brethren at Rome, with a pressing request for prayer:

Now I beseech you, brethren, for the Lord Jesus Christ's sake, and for the love of the Spirit, that ye strive together with me in your prayers to God for me; That I may be delivered from them that do not believe in Judea.

Their prayers, united with his prayer, were to secure his deliverance and secure his safety, and were also to make the apostolic promise vital and cause it to be fully realized.

All is to be sanctified and realized by the Word of God and prayer. God's deep and wide river of promise will turn into a deadly influence or be lost in the abyss, if we do not utilize these promises by prayer, and receive their full and life-giving waters into our hearts.

The promise of the Holy Spirit to the disciples was in a very marked way the "promise of the Father," but it was realized only after many days of continued and importunate praying. The promise was clear and definite that the disciples should be endued with power from on high, but as a condition of receiving that power of the Holy Spirit, they were instructed to "tarry in the city of Jerusalem till ye be endued with power from on high." The fulfillment of the promise depended upon the "tarrying." The promise of this "enduement of power" was made sure by prayer. Prayer sealed it to glorious results. So we find it written, "These continued with one accord, in prayer and supplication, with the women." And it is significant that it was while they were praying, resting their expectations on the surety of the promise, that the Holy Spirit fell upon them and they were all "filled with the Holy Spirit." The promise and the prayer went hand in hand.

After Jesus Christ made this large and definite promise to his disciples, he ascended on high, and was seated at his Father's right hand of exaltation and power. Yet the promise given by him of sending the Holy Spirit was not fulfilled by his enthronement merely, nor by the promise only, nor by the fact that the prophet Joel had foretold with transported raptures of the bright day of the Spirit's coming. Neither was it that the Spirit's coming was the only hope of God's cause in this world. All these all-powerful and all-engaging reasons were not the immediate operative cause of the coming of the Holy Spirit. The solution is found in the attitude of the disciples. The answer is found in the fact that the disciples, with the women, spent several days in that upper room, in earnest, specific, continued prayer. It was prayer that brought to pass the famous day of Pentecost. And as it was then, so it can be now. Prayer can bring a Pentecost in this day if there be the same kind of praying, for the promise has not exhausted its power and vitality. The "promise of the Father" still holds good for the present-day disciples.

Prayer, mighty prayer, united, continued, earnest prayer, for nearly two weeks, brought the Holy Spirit to the church and to the world in pentecostal glory and power. And mighty continued and united prayer will do the same now.

> Lord God, the Holy Ghost,
> In this accepted hour;

THE POSSIBILITIES OF PRAYER

> As on the day of Pentecost,
> Descend in all thy power.
> We meet with one accord,
> In our appointed place,
> And wait the promise of our Lord,
> The Spirit of all grace.

Nor must it be passed by that the promises of God to sinners of every kind and degree are equally sure and steadfast, and are made real and true by the earnest cries of all true penitents. It is just as true with the divine promises made to the unsaved when they repent and seek God, that they are realized in answer to the prayers of brokenhearted sinners, as it is true that the promises to believers are realized in answer to their prayers. The promise of pardon and peace was the basis of the prayers of Saul of Tarsus during those days of darkness and distress in the house of Judas, when the Lord told Ananias in order to allay his fears, "Behold he prayeth."

The promise of mercy and an abundant pardon is tied up with seeking God and calling upon him by Isaiah:

"Seek ye the Lord while he may be found, and call ye upon him while he is near. Let the wicked forsake his way and the unrighteous man his thoughts; and let him return unto the Lord, and he will have mercy, and to our God, for he will abundantly pardon."

The praying sinner receives mercy because his prayer is grounded on the promise of pardon made by him whose right it is to pardon guilty sinners. The penitent seeker after God obtains mercy because there is a definite promise of mercy to all who seek the Lord in repentance and faith. Prayer always brings forgiveness to the seeking soul. The abundant pardon is dependent upon the promise made real by the promise of God to the sinner.

While salvation is promised to him who believes, the believing sinner is always a praying sinner. God has no promise of pardon for a prayerless sinner just as he has no promise for the prayerless professor of religion. "Behold he prayeth" is not only the unfailing sign of sincerity and the evidence that the sinner is proceeding in the right way to find God, but it is also the unfailing prophecy of an abundant pardon. Get the sinner to praying according to the divine promise, and he then is near the kingdom of God. The very best sign of the returning prodigal is that he confesses his sins and begins to ask for the lowliest place in his father's house.

It is the divine promise of mercy, of forgiveness and of adoption which gives the poor sinner hope. This encourages him to pray. This moves him in distress to cry out, "Jesus, thou Son of David, have mercy upon me."

> Thy promise is my only plea,
> With this I venture nigh;
> Thou call'st the burdened soul to thee,
> And such, 0 Lord, am I.

How large are the promises made to the saint! How great the promises given to poor, hungry-hearted, lost sinners, ruined by the fall! And prayer has arms sufficient to encompass them all, and prove them. How great the encouragement to all souls, these promises of God! How firm the ground on which to rest our faith! How stimulating to prayer! What firm ground on which to base our pleas in praying!

> The Lord hath promised good to me,
> His word my hope secures;
> He will my shield and portion be
> As long as life endures.

4

Prayer—It's Possibilities

How vast are the possibilities of prayer! How wide is its reach! What great things are accomplished by this divinely appointed means of grace! It lays its hand on Almighty God and moves him to do what he would not otherwise do if prayer was not offered. It brings things to pass which would never otherwise occur. The story of prayer is the story of great achievements. Prayer is a wonderful power placed by Almighty God in the hands of his saints, which may be used to accomplish great purposes and to achieve unusual results. Prayer reaches to everything, takes in all things great and small which are promised by God to the children of men. The only limit to prayer are the promises of God and his ability to fulfill those promises. "Open thy mouth wide and I will fill it."

The records of prayer's achievements are encouraging to faith, cheering to the expectations of saints, and is an inspiration to all who would pray and test its value. Prayer is no mere untried theory. It is not some strange unique scheme, concocted in the brains of men, and set on foot by them, an invention which has never been tried nor put to the test. Prayer is a divine arrangement in the moral government of God, designed for the benefit of men and intended as a means for furthering the interests of his cause on earth, and carrying out his gracious purposes in redemption and providence. Prayer proves itself. It is susceptible of proving its virtue by those who pray. Prayer needs no proof other than its accomplishments. If any man will do his will, he shall know of the doctrine." If any man will know the virtue of prayer, if he will know what it will do, let him pray. Let him put prayer to the test.

What a breadth is given to prayer! What heights it reaches! It is the breathing of a soul inflamed for God, and inflamed for man. It goes as far as the gospel goes, and is as wide, compassionate, and prayerful as is that gospel.

How much of prayer do all these unpossessed, alienated provinces of earth demand to enlighten them, to impress them and to move them toward God and his Son, Jesus Christ? Had the professed disciples of Christ only have prayed in the past as they ought to have done, the centuries would not have found these provinces still bound in death, in sin, and in ignorance.

Alas! how the unbelief of men has limited the power of God to work through prayer! What limitations have disciples of Jesus Christ put upon prayer by their prayerlessness! How the church, with her neglect of prayer, has hedged about the gospel and shut up doors of access!

Prayer possibilities open doors for the entrance of the gospel: "Withal praying also for us that God would open to us a door of utterance." Prayer opened for the apostles doors of utterance, created opportunities and made openings to preach the gospel. The appeal by prayer was to God, because God was moved by prayer. God was thereby moved to do his own work in an enlarged way and by new ways. Prayer possibility gives not only great power, and opens doors to the gospel, but it gives facility as well to the gospel. Prayer makes the gospel to go fast and to move with glorious swiftness. A gospel projected by the mighty energies of prayer is neither slow, lazy nor dull. It moves with God's power, with God's radiance and with angelic swiftness.

"Brethren, pray for us that the word of the Lord may have free course and be glorified," is the request of the apostle Paul, whose faith reached to the possibilities of prayer for the preached Word. The gospel moves altogether too slowly, often timidly, idly, and with feeble steps. What will make this gospel go rapidly like a race runner? What will give this gospel divine radiance and glory, and cause it to move worthy of God and of Christ? The answer is at hand. Prayer, more prayer, better prayer will do the deed. This means of grace will give fast going, splendor, and divinity to the gospel.

The possibilities of prayer reach to all things. Whatever concerns man's highest welfare, and whatever has to do with God's plans and purposes concerning men on earth, is a subject for prayer. In "whatsoever ye shall ask," is embraced all that concerns us or the children of men and God. And whatever is left out of "whatsoever" is left out of prayer. Where will we draw the lines which leave out or which will limit the word "whatsoever"? Define it, and search out and publish the things which the word does not include. If "whatsoever" does not include all things, then add to it the word "anything." "If ye shall ask anything in my name, I will do it."

What riches of grace, what blessings, spiritual and temporal, what good for time and eternity, would have been ours had we learned the possibilities of prayer and our faith had taken in the wide range of the divine promises to us to answer prayer! What blessings on our times and what furtherance to God's cause had we but learned how to pray with large expectations! Who will rise up in this generation and teach the church this lesson? It is a child's lesson in simplicity, but who has learned it well enough to put prayer to the test? It is a great lesson in its matchless and universal good. The possibilities of prayer are unspeakable, but the lesson of prayer which realizes and measures up to these possibilities, who has learned?

In his discourse in John fifteen, our Lord seems to connect friendship for him with prayer, and his choosing of his disciples seemed to have been with a design that through prayer they should bear much fruit.

"Ye are my friends if ye do whatsoever I command you. Ye have not chosen me, but I have chosen you, and ordained you, that ye should go and bring forth fruit, and that your fruit should remain; that whatsoever ye shall ask the Father in my name, he may give it to you."

Here we have again the undefined and unlimited word, "whatsoever," as covering the rights and the things for which we are to pray in the possibilities of prayer.

We have still another declaration from Jesus:

"Verily, verily, I say unto you, Whatsoever ye shall ask the Father in my name, he will give it to you. Hitherto ye have asked nothing in my name; ask, and ye shall receive, that your joy may be full."

Here is a very definite exhortation from our Lord to largeness in praying. Here we are definitely urged by him to ask for large things, and announced with the dignity and solemnity indicated by the double amen, "Verily, Verily." Why these marvelous urgencies in this last recorded and vital conversation of our Lord with his disciples? The answer is that our Lord might prepare them for the new dispensation, in which prayer was to have such marvelous results, and in which prayer was to be the chief agency to conserve and make aggressive his gospel.

In our Lord's language to his disciples about choosing them that should bear fruit, he clearly teaches us that this matter of praying and fruit-bearing is not a petty business of our choice, or a secondary matter in relation to other matters, but that he has chosen us for this very business of praying. He had specially in mind our praying, and he has chosen us of his own divine selection, and he expects us to do this one thing of praying and to do it intelligently and well. For he before says that he had made us his friends, and had brought us into bosom confidence with him, and also into free and full conference with him. The main object of choosing us as his disciples and of friendship for him was that we might be the better fitted to bear the fruit of prayer.

Let us not forget that we are noting the possibilities of the true praying ones. "Anything" is the word of area and circumference. How far it reaches we may not know. How wide it spreads, our minds fail to discover. What is there which is not within its reach? Why does Jesus repeat and exhaust these words, all-inclusive and boundless words, if he does not desire to emphasize the unbounded magnificence and illimitable munificence of prayer? Why does he press men to pray, so that our very poverty might be enriched and our limitless inheritance by prayer be secured?

We affirm with absolute certainty that Almighty God answers prayer. The vast possibilities, and the urgent necessity of prayer lie in this stupendous fact that God hears and answers prayer. And God hears and answers all prayer. He hears and answers every prayer, where the true conditions of praying are met.Either this is so or it is not. If not, then is there nothing in prayer. Then prayer is but the recitation of words, a mere verbal performance, an empty ceremony. Then prayer is an altogether useless exercise. But if what we have said is true, then are there vast possibilities in prayer. Then is it far reaching in its scope, and wide in its range. Then is it true that prayer can lay its hand upon Almighty God and move him to do great and wonderful things.

The benefits, the possibilities and the necessity of prayer are not merely subjective but are peculiarly objective in their character. Prayer aims at a definite object. Prayer has a direct design in view. Prayer always has something specific before the mind's eye. There may be some subjective benefits which accrue from praying, but this is altogether secondary and incidental. Prayer always drives directly at an object and seeks to secure a desired end. Prayer is asking, seeking and knocking at a door for something we have not, which we desire, and which God has promised to us.

Prayer is a direct address to God. "In everything let your requests be made known unto God." Prayer secures blessings, and makes men better because it reaches the ear of God. Prayer is only for the betterment of men when it has affected God and moved him to do something for men. Prayer affects men by affecting God. Prayer moves men because it moves God to move men. Prayer influences men by influencing God to influence them. Prayer moves the hand that moves the world.

That power is prayer, which soars on high,
Through Jesus to the throne;
And moves the hand which moves the world,
To bring salvation down.

The utmost possibilities of prayer have rarely been realized. The promises of God are so great to those who truly pray, when he puts himself so fully into the hands of the praying ones, that it almost staggers our faith and causes us to hesitate with astonishment. His promise to answer, and to do and to give "all things," "anything," "whatsoever," and "all things whatsoever," is so large, so great, so exceeding broad, that we stand back in amazement and give ourselves to questioning and doubt. We "stagger at the promises through unbelief." Really the answers of God to prayer have been pared down by us to our little faith, and have been brought down to the low level of our narrow notions about God's ability, liberality, and resources. Let us ever keep in mind and never for one moment allow ourselves to doubt the statement that God means what he says in all of his promises. God's promises are his own word. His veracity is at stake in them. To question them is to doubt his veracity. He cannot afford to prove faithless to his word. "In hope of eternal life, which God that cannot lie, promised before the world began." His promises are for plain people, and he means to do for all who pray just what he says he will do. "For he is faithful that hath promised."

Unfortunately we have failed to lay ourselves out in praying. We have limited the Holy One of Israel. The ability to pray can be secured by the grace and power of the Holy Spirit, but it demands so strenuous and high a character that it is a rare thing for a man or woman to be on "praying ground and on pleading terms with God." It is as true today as it was in the days of Elijah, that "the fervent, effectual prayer of a righteous man availeth much." How much such a prayer avails, who can tell?

The possibilities of prayer are the possibilities of faith. Prayer and faith are Siamese twins. One heart animates them both. Faith is always praying. Prayer is always believing. Faith must have a tongue by which it can speak. Prayer is the tongue of faith. Faith must receive. Prayer is the hand of faith stretched out to receive. Prayer must rise and soar. Faith must give prayer the wings to fly and soar. Prayer must have an audience with God. Faith opens the door, and access and audience are given. Prayer asks. Faith lays its hand on the thing asked for.

God's omnipotent power is the basis of omnipotent faith and omnipotent praying. "All things are possible to him that believeth," and "all things whatsoever" are given to him who prays. God's decree and death yield readily to Hezekiah's faith and prayer. When God's promise and man's praying are united by faith, then "nothing shall be impossible." Importunate prayer is so all powerful and irresistible that it obtains promises, or wins where the prospect and the promise seem to be against it. In fact, the New Testament promise includes all things in heaven and in earth. God, by promise, puts all things he possesses into man's hands. Prayer and faith put man in possession of this boundless inheritance.

Prayer is not an indifferent or a small thing. It is not a sweet little privilege. It is a great prerogative, far-reaching in its effects. Failure to pray entails losses far beyond the person who neglects it. Prayer is not a mere episode of the Christian life. Rather the whole life is a preparation for and the result of prayer. In its condition, prayer is the sum of religion. Faith is but a channel of prayer. Faith gives it wings and swiftness. Prayer is the lungs through which holiness breathes. Prayer is not only the language of spiritual life, but also makes its very essence and forms its real character.

> O for a faith that will not shrink
> Though pressed by every foe;
> That will not tremble on the brink
> Of any earthly woe.

Lord, give us such a faith as this,
And then, whate'er may come,
We'll taste e'en here, the hallowed bliss
Of our eternal home.

5

Prayer—It's Possibilities (Continued)

AFTER a comprehensive and cursory view of the possibilities of prayer, as mapped out in what has been said, it is important to descend to particulars, to Bible facts and principles in regard to this great subject. What are the possibilities of prayer as disclosed by divine revelation? The necessity of prayer and its being are coexistent with man. Nature, even before a clear and full revelation, cries out in prayer. Man is, therefore prayer is. God is, therefore prayer is. Prayer is born of the instincts, the needs and the cravings and the very being of man.

The prayer of Solomon at the dedication of the temple is the product of inspired wisdom and piety, and gives a lucid and powerful view of prayer in the wideness of its range, the minuteness of its details, and its abounding possibilities and its urgent necessity. How minute and exactly comprehending is this prayer! National and individual blessings are in it, and temporal and spiritual good is embraced by it. Individual sins, national calamities, sins, sickness, exile, famine, war, pestilence, mildew, drought, insects, damage to crops, whatever affects husbandry, enemies-whatsoever sickness, one's own sore, one's own guilt, one's own sin-one and all are in this prayer, and all are for prayer.

For all these evils prayer is the one universal remedy. Pure praying remedies all ills, cures all diseases, relieves all situations, however dire, calamitous, fearful, and despairing. Prayer to God, pure praying, relieves dire situations because God can relieve when no one else can. Nothing is too hard for God. No cause is hopeless which God undertakes. No case is mortal when Almighty God is the physician. No conditions are despairing which can deter or defy God.

Almighty God heard this prayer of Solomon, and committed himself to undertake, to relieve and to remedy if real praying be done, despite all adverse and inexorable conditions. He will always relieve, answer and bless if men will pray from the heart, and if they will give themselves to real, true praying.

This is the record of what God said to him after Solomon had finished his magnificent, illimitable and all-comprehending prayer:

"And the Lord appeared to Solomon by night, and said to him, I have heard thy prayer, and have chosen this place to myself for a house of sacrifice. If I shut up heaven that there be no rain, or if I command the locusts that they devour the land, or if I send pestilence among the people; If my people which are called by my name, shall humble themselves and pray, and seek my face, and turn from their wicked ways, then will I hear from heaven, and will forgive their sin, and will heal their land; Now my eyes shall be open, and my ears attentive to the prayer that is made in this place. For now I have chosen and sanctified this house, that my name may be there forever."

God put no limitation to his ability to save through true praying. No hopeless conditions, no accumulation of difficulties, and no desperation in distance or circumstance can hinder the success of real prayer. The possibilities of prayer are linked to the infinite integrity and omnipotent power of God. There is nothing too hard for God to do. God is pledged that if we ask, we shall receive. God can withhold nothing from faith and prayer.

> The thing surpasses all my thought,
> But faithful is my Lord;
> Through unbelief I stagger not,

For God hath spoke the word.
Faith, mighty faith, the promise sees,
And looks to that alone;
Laughs at impossibilities,
And cries, "It shall be done!"

The many statements of God's Word fully set forth the possibilities and far reaching nature of prayer. How full of pathos! Call upon me in the day of trouble; I will deliver thee, and thou shalt glorify me." Again, read the cheering words: "He shall call upon me, and I will answer him; I will be with him in trouble; I will deliver him and honor him."

How diversified the range of trouble! How almost infinite its extent! How universal and dire its conditions! How despairing its waves! Yet the range of prayer is as great as trouble, is as universal as sorrow, as infinite as grief. And prayer can relieve all these evils which come to the children of men. There is no tear which prayer cannot wipe away or dry up. There is no depression of spirits which it cannot relieve and elevate. There is no despair which it cannot dispel.

"Call unto me, and I will answer thee, and show thee great things and difficult, which thou knowest not." How broad these words of the Lord, how great the promise, how cheering to faith! They really challenge the faith of the saint. Prayer always brings God to our relief to bless and to aid, and brings marvelous revelations of his power. What impossibilities are there with God? Name them. "Nothing," he says, "is impossible to the Lord." And all the possibilities in God are in prayer.

Samuel, under the judges of Israel, will fully illustrate the possibility and the necessity of prayer. He himself was the beneficiary of the greatness of faith and prayer in a mother who knew what praying meant. Hannah, his mother, was a woman of mark, in character and in piety, who was childless. That privation was a source of worry and weakness and grief. She sought God for relief, and prayed and poured out her soul before the Lord. She continued her praying, in fact she multiplied her praying, to such an extent that to old Eli she seemed to be intoxicated, almost beside herself in the intensity of her supplications. She was specific in her prayers. She wanted a child. For a man child she prayed.

And God was specific in his answer. A man child God gave her, a man indeed he became. He was the creation of prayer, and grew himself to a man of prayer. He was a mighty intercessor, especially in emergencies in the history of God's people. The epitome of his life and character is found in the statement, "Samuel cried unto the Lord for Israel, and the Lord heard him." The victory was complete, and the ebenezer was the memorial of the possibilities and necessity of prayer.

Again, at another time, Samuel called to the Lord, and thunder and rain came out of season in wheat harvest. Here are some statements concerning this mighty intercessor, who knew how to pray, and whom God always regarded when he prayed: "Samuel cried unto the Lord all night."

Says he at another time in speaking to the Lord's people, "Moreover, as for me, God forbid that I should sin against the Lord in ceasing to pray for you."

These great occasions show how this notable ruler of Israel made prayer a habit, and that this was a notable and conspicuous characteristic of his dispensation. Prayer was no strange exercise to Samuel. He was accustomed to it. He was in the habit of praying, knew the way to God, and received answers from God. Through Samuel and his praying God's cause was brought out of its low, depressed condition, and a great national revival began, of which David was one of its fruits.

Samuel was one of the notable men of the old dispensation who stood out prominently as one who had great influence with God in prayer. God could not deny Samuel anything he asked of God. Samuel's praying always affected God, and moved God to do what would not have otherwise been done had Samuel not prayed. Samuel stands out as a striking illustration of the possibilities of prayer. He shows conclusively the achievements of prayer.

Jacob is an illustration for all time of the commanding and conquering forces of prayer. God came to him as an antagonist. He grappled

Jacob, and shook him as if he were in the embrace of a deadly foe. Jacob, the deceitful supplanter, the wily, unscrupulous trader, had no eyes to see God. His perverted principles, and his deliberate overreaching and wrongdoing had blinded his vision.

To reach God, to know God, and to conquer God, was the demand of this critical hour. Jacob was alone, and all night witnessed to the intensity of the struggle, its changing issues, and its veering fortunes, as well as the receding and advancing lines in the conflict. Here was the strength of weakness, the power of self-despair, the energy of perseverance, the elevation of humility, and the victory of surrender. Jacob's salvation issued from the forces which he massed in that all-night conflict.

He prayed and wept and importuned until the fiery hate of Esau's heart died and it was softened into love. A greater miracle was wrought on Jacob than on Esau. His name, his character, and his destiny were changed by that all-night praying. Here is the record of the results of that night's praying struggle: "As a prince hast thou power with God and with men, and hast prevailed." "By his strength he had power with God, yea, he had power over the angel and prevailed."

What forces lie in importunate prayer! What mighty results are gained by it in one night's struggle in praying! God is affected and changed in attitude, and two men are transformed in character and destiny.

6

Prayer—It's Possibilities (Continued)

THE possibilities of prayer are seen in its results in temporal matters. Prayer reaches to everything which concerns man, whether it be his body, his mind, or his soul. Prayer embraces the very smallest things of life. Prayer takes in the wants of the body, food, raiment, business, finances, in fact everything which belongs to this life, as well as those things which have to do with the eternal interests of the soul. Its achievements are seen not only in the large things of earth, but more especially in what might be called the little things of life. It brings to pass not only large things, speaking after the manner of men, but also the small things.

Temporal matters are of a lower order than the spiritual, but they concern us greatly. Our temporal interests make up a great part of our lives. They are the main source of our cares and worries. They have much to do with our religion. We have bodies, with wants, pains, disabilities, and limitations. That which concerns our bodies necessarily engages our minds. These are subjects of prayer, and prayer takes in all of them, and large are the accomplishments of prayer in this realm of our being.

Our temporal matters have much to do with our health and happiness. They form our relations. They are tests of honesty and belong to the sphere of justice and righteousness. Not to pray about temporal matters is to leave God out of the largest sphere of our being. He who cannot pray in everything, as we are charged to do by Paul in Philippians, fourth chapter, has never learned in any true sense the nature and worth of prayer. To leave business and time out of prayer is to leave religion and eternity out of it. He who does not pray about temporal matters cannot pray with confidence about spiritual matters. He who does not put God by prayer in his struggling toil for daily bread will never put him in his struggle for heaven. He who does not cover and supply the wants of the body by prayer will never cover and supply the wants of his soul. Both body and soul are dependent on God, and prayer is but the crying expression of that dependence.

The Syrophoenician woman prayed for the health things. In fact the Old Testament is but the record of God in dealing with his people through the divine appointment of prayer. Abraham prayed that Sodom might be saved from destruction. Abraham's servant prayed and received God's direction in choosing a wife for Isaac. Hannah prayed, and Samuel was given to her. Elijah prayed, and no rain came for three years. And he prayed again, and the clouds gave rain. Hezekiah was saved from a mortal sickness by his praying. Jacob's praying saved him from Esau's revenge. The old Bible is the history of prayer for temporal blessings as well as for spiritual blessings.

In the New Testament we have the same principles illustrated and enforced. Prayer in this section of God's Word covers the whole realm of good, both temporal and spiritual. Our Lord, in his universal prayer, the prayer for humanity, in every clime, in every age and for every condition, puts in it the petition, "Give us this day our daily bread." This embraces all necessary earthly good.

In the Sermon on the Mount, a whole paragraph is taken up by our Lord about food and raiment, where he is cautioning against undue care or anxiety for these things, and at the same time encouraging a faith which takes in and claims all these necessary bodily comforts and necessities. And this teaching stands in close connection with his teachings about prayer. Food and raiment are taught as subjects of prayer. Not for one moment is it even hinted that they are things beneath the notice of a great God, nor too material and earthly for such a spiritual exercise as prayer.

The Syrophoenician woman prayed for the health of her daughter. Peter prayed for Dorcas to be brought back to life. Paul prayed for the father of Publius on his way to Rome, when cast on the island by a shipwreck, and God healed the man who was sick with a fever. He urged the Christians at Rome to strive with him together in prayer that he might be delivered from bad men.

When Peter was put in prison by Herod, the church was instant in prayer that Peter might be delivered from the prison, and God honored the praying of these early Christians. John prayed that Gaius might "prosper and be in health, even as his soul prospered."

The divine directory in James, fifth chapter, says: "Is any among you afflicted, let him pray Is any sick among you? Let him call for the elders of the church, and let them pray over him."

Paul, in writing to the Philippians, fourth chapter, says: "Be careful for nothing; but in everything, by prayer and supplication, with thanksgiving, let your requests be made known to God." This provides for all kinds of cares-business cares, home cares, body cares, and soul cares. All are to be brought to God by prayer, and at the mercy seat our minds and souls are to be unburdened of all that affects us or causes anxiety or uneasiness. These words of Paul stand in close connection with what he says about temporal matters specially: "But now I rejoiced in the Lord greatly that now at the last your care of me bath flourished-again: wherein ye were also careful, but ye lacked opportunity. Not that I speak in respect to want, for I have learned in whatsoever state I am, therewith to be content."

And Paul closes his epistle to these Christians with the words, which embrace all temporal needs as well as spiritual wants:

But my God shall supply all your need, according to his riches in glory, by Christ Jesus.

Unbelief in the doctrine that prayer covers all things which have to do with the body and business affairs, breeds undue anxiety about earth's affairs, causes unnecessary worry, and creates very unhappy states of mind. How much needless care we would save ourselves if we but believed in prayer as the means of relieving those cares, and would learn the happy art of casting all our cares in prayer upon God, "who careth for us!" Unbelief in God as one who is concerned about even the smallest affairs which affect our happiness and comfort limits the holy one of Israel, and makes our lives altogether devoid of real happiness and sweet contentment.

We have in the instance of the failure of the disciples to cast the devil out of the lunatic son, brought to them by his father, while Jesus was on the Mount of Transfiguration, a suggestive lesson of the union of faith, prayer, and fasting, and the failure to reach the possibilities and obligations of an occasion. The disciples ought to have cast the devil out of the boy. They had been sent out to do this very work, and had been empowered by their Lord and master to do it. And yet they signally failed. Christ reproved them with sharp upbraidings for not doing it. They had been sent out on this very specific mission. This one thing was specified by our Lord when he sent them out. Their failure brought shame and confusion on them, and discounted their Lord and master and his cause. They brought him into disrepute, and reflected very seriously upon the cause which they represented. Their faith to cast out the devil had signally failed, simply because it had not been nurtured by prayer and fasting. Failure to pray broke the ability of faith, and failure came because they had not the energy of a strong authoritative faith.

The promise reads, and we cannot too often refer to it, for it is the very basis of our faith and the ground on which we stand when we pray: "All things whatsoever ye ask in prayer, believing, ye shall receive." What enumeration table can tabulate, itemize, and aggregate "all things whatsoever"? The possibilities of prayer and faith go to the length of the endless chain, and cover the unmeasurable area.

In Hebrews eleven, the sacred penman, wearied with trying to specify the examples of faith, and to recite the wonderful exploits of faith, pauses a moment, and then cries out, giving us almost unheard of achievements of prayer and faith as exemplified by the saints of the olden times. Here is what he says:

And what shall I say more? For the time would fail me to tell of Gideon, of Barak, of Samson, of Jephthah, of David also; and Samuel, and the prophets; Who through faith, subdued kingdoms, wrought righteousness, obtained promises, stopped the mouths of lions; Quenched the violence of fire, escaped the edge of the sword, out of weakness were made strong, waxed valiant in fight, turned to flight the armies of the aliens; Women received their dead raised to life again, and others were tortured, not accepting deliverance; that they might obtain a better resurrection.

What an illustrious record is this! What marvelous accomplishments, wrought not by armies, or by man's superhuman strength, nor by magic, but all accomplished simply by men and women noted alone for their faith and prayer! Hand in hand with these records of faith's illimitable range are the illustrious records of prayer, for they are all one. Faith has never won a victory nor gained a crown where prayer was not the weapon of the victory, and where prayer did not jewel the crown. If "all things are possible to him that believeth," then all things are possible to him that prays.

> Depend on him; thou canst not fail;
> Make all thy wants and wishes known:
> Fear not; his merits must prevail;
> Ask but in faith, it shall be done.

7

Prayer—It's Wide Range

THE possibilities of prayer are gauged by faith in God's ability to do. Faith is the one prime condition by which God works. Faith is the one prime condition by which man prays. Faith draws on God to its full extent. Faith gives character to prayer. A feeble faith has always brought forth feeble praying. Vigorous faith creates vigorous praying. At the close of a parable, "And he spake a parable unto them to this end, that men always ought to pray, and not to faint," in which he stressed the necessity of vigorous praying, Christ asks this pointed question, "When the Son of Man cometh, shall he find faith on the earth?"

In the case of the lunatic child which the father brought first to the disciples, who could not cure him, and then to the Lord Jesus Christ, the father cried out with all the pathos of a declining faith and of a great sorrow, "If thou canst do anything for us, have compassion on us and help us." And Jesus said unto him, "If thou canst believe, all things are possible to him that believeth." The healing turned on the faith in the ability of Christ to heal the boy. The ability to do was in Christ essentially and eternally, but the doing of the thing turned on the ability of the faith. Great faith enables Christ to do great things.

We need a quickening faith in God's power. We have hedged God in till we have little faith in his power. We have conditioned the exercise of his power till we have a little God, and a little faith in a little God.

The only condition which restrains God's power, and which disables him to act, is unfaith. He is not limited in action nor restrained by the conditions which limit men.

The conditions of time, place, nearness, ability, and all others which could possibly be named, upon which the actions of men hinge, have no bearing on God. If men will look to God and cry to him with true prayer, he will hear and can deliver, no matter how dire may be their state, how remediless their conditions may be.

Strange how God has to school his people in his ability to do! He made a promise to Abraham and Sarah that Isaac would be born. Abraham was then nearly one hundred years old, and Sarah was barren by natural defect, and had passed into a barren age. She laughed at the preposterous thought of having a child. God asked, "Why did Sarah laugh? Is anything too hard for the Lord?" And God fulfilled his promise to these old people to the letter.

Moses hesitated to undertake God's purpose to liberate Israel from Egyptian bondage, because of his inability to talk well. God checks him at once by an inquiry:

And Moses said unto the Lord, 0 my Lord, I am not eloquent, neither heretofore, nor since thou hast spoken unto thy servant; but I am slow of speech and of a slow tongue. And the Lord said unto him, Who hath made man's mouth? or who maketh the dumb, or deaf, or the seeing, or the blind? Have not I the Lord? Now, therefore, go, and I will be with thy mouth, and teach thee what thou shalt say.

When God said he would feed the children of Israel a whole month with meat, Moses questioned his ability to do it. The Lord said unto Moses, "Is the Lord's hand waxed short? Thou shalt see now whether my word shall come to pass unto thee or not."

Nothing is too hard for the Lord to do. As Paul declared, "He is able to do exceeding abundantly above all that we can ask or think." Prayer has to do with God, with his ability to do. The possibility of prayer is the measure of God's ability to do.

The "all things," the "all things whatsoever," and the "anything," are all covered by the ability of God. The urgent entreaty reads, "Ask whatsoever ye will," because God is able to do anything and all things that my desires may crave, and that he has promised. In God's ability to do, he goes far beyond man's ability to ask. Human thoughts, human words, human imaginations, human desires, and human needs cannot in any way measure God's ability to do.

Prayer in its legitimate possibilities goes out on God himself. Prayer goes out with faith not only in the promise of God, but also faith in God himself, and in God's ability to do. Prayer goes out not on the promise merely, but "obtains promises," and creates promises.

Elijah had the promise that God would send the rain, but no promise that he would send the fire. But by faith and prayer he obtained the fire, as well as the rain, but the fire came first.

Daniel had no specific promise that God would make known to him the dream of the king, but he and his associates joined in united prayer, and God revealed to Daniel the king's dream and the interpretation, and their lives were spared thereby.

Hezekiah had no promise that God would cure him of his desperate sickness which threatened his life. On the contrary, the word of the Lord came to him by the mouth of the prophet, that he should die. However, he prayed against this decree of Almighty God, with faith, and he succeeded in obtaining a reversal of God's word and lived.

God makes it marvelous when he says by the mouth of his prophet: "Thus saith the Lord, the Holy One of Israel and his Maker: Ask me of things to come, concerning my sons, and concerning the work of my hands, command ye me." And in this strong promise in which he commits himself into the hands of his praying people, he appeals in it to his great creative power: "I have created the earth and made man upon it. I, even my hands, have stretched out the heavens, and all their hosts have I commanded."

The majesty and power of God in making man and man's world, and constantly upholding all things, are ever kept before us as the basis of our faith in God, and as an assurance and urgency to prayer. Then God calls us away from what he himself has done, and turns our minds to himself personally. The infinite glory and power of his person are set before our contemplation: "Remember ye not the former things neither consider the things of old?" He declares that he will do a "new thing," that he does not have to repeat himself, that all he has done neither limits his doing nor the manner of his doing, and that if we have prayer and faith, he will so answer our prayers and so work for us, that his former work shall not be remembered nor come into mind. If men would pray as they ought to pray, the marvels of the past would be more than reproduced. The gospel would advance with a facility and power it has never known. Doors would be thrown open to the gospel, and the Word of God would have a conquering force rarely, if ever, known before.

If Christians prayed as Christians ought, with strong commanding faith, with earnestness and sincerity, men, God-called men, God-empowered men everywhere, would be all burning to go and spread the gospel worldwide. The Word of the Lord would run and be glorified as never known heretofore. The God-influenced men, the God-inspired men, the God-commissioned men, would go and kindle the flame of sacred fire for Christ, salvation and heaven, everywhere in all nations, and soon all people would hear the glad tidings of salvation and have an opportunity to receive Jesus Christ as their personal savior. Let us read another one of those large illimitable statements in God's Word, which are a direct challenge to prayer and faith:

He that spared not his own Son, but delivered him up for us all, how shall he not with him freely give us all things?

What a basis have we here for prayer and faith, illimitable, measureless in breadth, in depth, and in height! The promise to give us all things is backed up by the calling to our remembrance of the fact that God freely gave his only begotten Son for our redemption. God giving his Son is the assurance and guarantee that he will freely give all things to him who believes and prays.

What confidence have we in this divine statement for inspired asking! What holy boldness we have here for the largest asking! No commonplace tameness should restrain our largest asking. Large, larger, and largest asking magnifies grace and adds to God's glory. Feeble asking impoverishes the asker, and restrains God's purposes for the greatest good and obscures his glory.

How enthroned, magnificent, and royal the intercession of our Lord Jesus Christ at his Father's right hand in heaven! The benefits of his intercession flow to us through our intercessions. Our intercession ought to catch by contagion, and by necessity the inspiration and largeness of Christ's great work at his Father's right hand. His business and his life are to pray. Our business and our lives ought to be to pray, and to pray without ceasing.

Failure in our intercession affects the fruits of his intercession. Lazy, heartless, feeble, and indifferent praying by us mars and hinders the effects of Christ's praying.

8

Prayer—Facts and History

THE possibilities of prayer are established by the facts and the history of prayer. Facts are stubborn things. Facts are the true things. Theories may be but speculations. Opinions may be wholly at fault. But facts must be deferred to. They cannot be ignored. What are the possibilities of prayer judged by the facts? What is the history of prayer? What does it reveal to us? Prayer has a history, written in God's Word and recorded in the experiences and lives of God's saints. History is truth teaching by example. We may miss the truth by perverting the history, but the truth is in the facts of history.

> He spake with Abraham at the oak,
> He called Elisha from the plough;
> David he from the sheepfolds took,
> Thy day, thine hour of grace, is now.

God reveals the truth by the facts. God reveals himself by the facts of religious history. God teaches us his will by the facts and examples of Bible history. God's facts, God's Word, and God's history are all in perfect harmony, and have much of God in them all. God has ruled the world by prayer; and God still rules the world by the same divinely ordained means.

THE POSSIBILITIES OF PRAYER

The possibilities of prayer cover not only individuals but also reach to cities and nations. They take in classes and peoples. The praying of Moses was the one thing which stood between the wrath of God against the Israelites and his declared purpose to destroy them and the execution of that divine purpose, and the Hebrew nation still survived. Notwithstanding Sodom was not spared, because ten righteous men could not be found inside its limits, yet the little city of Zoar was spared because Lot prayed for it as he fled from the storm of fire and brimstone which burned up Sodom. Nineveh was saved because the king and its people repented of their evil ways and gave themselves to prayer and fasting.

Paul in his remarkable prayer in Ephesians, chapter three, honors the illimitable possibilities of prayer and glorifies the ability of God to answer prayer. Closing that memorable prayer, so far-reaching in its petitions, and setting forth the very deepest religious experience, he declares that "God is able to do exceeding abundantly above all that we can ask or think." He makes prayer all-inclusive, comprehending all things, great and small. There is no time nor place which prayer does not cover and sanctify. All things in earth and in heaven, everything for time and for eternity, all are embraced in prayer. Nothing is too great and nothing is too small to be subject of prayer. Prayer reaches down to the least things of life and includes the greatest things which concern us.

> If pain afflict or wrongs oppress,
> If cares distract, or fears dismay;
> If guilt deject, or sin distress,
> In every case still watch and pray.

One of the most important, far-reaching, peace-giving, necessary, and practical prayer possibilities we have in Paul's words in Philippians, chapter four, dealing with prayer as a cure for undue care:

Be careful for nothing; but in everything, by prayer and supplication, with thanksgiving, let your requests be made known unto God. And the peace of God which passeth all understanding shall keep your hearts and minds through Christ Jesus.

"Cares" are the epidemic evil of mankind. They are universal in their reach. They belong to man in his fallen condition. The predisposition to undue anxiety is the natural result of sin. Care comes in all shapes, at all times, and from all sources. It comes to all of every age and station. There are the cares of the home circle, from which there is no escape save in prayer. There are the cares of business, the cares of poverty, and the cares of riches. Ours is an anxious world, and ours is an anxious race. The caution of Paul is well addressed, "In nothing be anxious." This is the divine injunction, and that we might be able to live above anxiety and freed from undue care, "In everything, by prayer and supplication, let your requests be made known unto God." This is the divinely prescribed remedy for all anxious cares, for all worry, for all inward fretting.

The word careful means to be drawn in different directions, distracted, anxious, disturbed, annoyed in spirit. Jesus had warned against this very thing in the Sermon on the Mount, where he had earnestly urged his disciples, "Take no thought for the morrow," in things concerning the needs of the body. He was endeavoring to show them the true secret of a quiet mind, freed from anxiety and unnecessary care about food and raiment. Tomorrow's evils were not to be considered. He was simply teaching the same lesson found in Psalm 37:3, "Trust in the Lord, and do good; so shalt thou dwell in the land, and verily thou shalt be fed." In cautioning against the fears of tomorrow's prospective evils, and the material wants of the body, our Lord was teaching the great lesson of an implicit and childlike confidence in God. "Commit thy way unto the Lord: trust also in him, and he shall bring it to pass."

> "Day by day," the promise reads,
> Daily strength for daily needs
> Cast foreboding fears away;
> Take the manna of today.

Paul's direction is very specific, "Be careful for nothing." Be careful for not one thing. Be careful for not anything, for any condition, chance, or happening. Be troubled about not anything which creates one disturbing anxiety. Have a mind freed from all anxieties, all cares, all fretting, and all worries. Cares divide, distract, bewilder, and destroy unity, power, and quietness of mind. Cares are fatal to weak piety and are enfeebling to strong piety. What great need to guard against them and learn the one secret of their cure, even prayer!

What boundless possibilities there are in prayer to remedy the situation of mind of which Paul is speaking! Prayer over everything can quiet every distraction, hush every anxiety, and lift every care from care-enslaved lives and from care-bewildered hearts. The prayer specific is the perfect cure for all ills of this character which belong to anxieties, cares, and worries. Only prayer in everything can drive dull care away, relieve unnecessary heart burdens, and save from the besetting sin of worrying over things which we cannot help. Only prayer can bring into the heart and mind the "peace which passeth all understanding," and keep mind and heart at ease, free from burdensome care.

Oh, the needless heart burdens borne by fretting Christians! How few know the real secret of a happy Christian life, filled with perfect peace, hid from the storms and billows of a fretting careworn life! Prayer has a possibility of saving us from carefulness, the bane of human lives. Paul in writing to the Corinthians says, "I would have you without carefulness," and this is the will of God. Prayer has the ability to do this very thing. "Casting all your care on him, for he careth for you," is the way Peter puts it, while the psalmist says, "Fret not thyself in any wise to do evil." Oh, the blessedness of a heart at ease from all inward care, exempt from undue anxiety, in the enjoyment of the peace of God which passeth all understanding!

Paul's injunction which includes both God's promise and his purpose, and which immediately precedes his entreaty to be "careful for nothing," reads on this wise:

> Rejoice in the Lord always,
> and again I say, Rejoice.
> Let your moderation be made known to all men.
> The Lord is at hand.

In a world filled with cares of every kind, where temptation is the rule, where there are so many things to try us, how is it possible to rejoice always? We look at the naked, dry command, and we accept it and reverence it as the Word of God, but no joy comes. How are we to let our moderation, our mildness, and our gentleness be universally and always known? We resolve to be benign and gentle. We remember the nearness of the Lord, but still we are hasty, quick, hard, and salty. We listen to the divine charge, "Be careful for nothing," yet still we are anxious, care-worn, care-eaten, and care-tossed. How can we fulfill the divine word, so sweet and so large in promise, so beautiful in the eye, and yet so far from being realized? How can we enter upon the rich patrimony of being true, honest, just, pure, and possess lovely things? The recipe is infallible, the remedy is universal, and the cure is unfailing. It is found in the words which we have so often herein referred to of Paul: "Be careful for nothing, but in everything, by prayer and supplication, with thanksgiving, let your requests be made known unto God."

This joyous, care-free, peaceful experience bringing the believer into a joyousness, living simply by faith day by day, is the will of God. Writing to the Thessalonians, Paul tells them: "Rejoice evermore; pray without ceasing, and in everything give thanks, for this is the will of God in Christ Jesus concerning you." So that not only is it God's will that we should find full deliverance from all care and undue anxiety, but he has also ordained prayer as the means by which we can reach that happy state of heart.

The Revised Version makes some changes in the passage of Paul, about which we have been speaking. The reading there is "In nothing be anxious," and "the peace of God shall guard your hearts and your minds." And Paul puts the antecedent in the air of prayer, which is "Rejoice in the Lord always." That is, be always glad in the Lord, and be happy with him. And that you may thus be happy, "Be careful for nothing." This rejoicing is the doorway for prayer, and its pathway, too. The sunshine and buoyancy of joy in the Lord are the strength and boldness of prayer, the means of its victory. "Moderation" makes the rainbow of prayer. The word means mildness, fairness, gentleness, sweet reasonableness. The Revised Version changes it to "forbearance," with the margin reading "gentleness." What rare ingredients and beautiful colorings! These are colorings and ingredients which make a strong and beautiful character and a wide and positive reputation. A rejoicing, gentle spirit, positive in reputation, is well fitted for prayer, rid of the distractions and unrest of care.

9

Prayer—Facts and History (Continued)

IT is to the closet Paul directs us to go. The unfailing remedy for all burdensome, distressing care is prayer. The place where the Lord is at hand is the closet of prayer. There he is always found, and there he is at hand to bless, to deliver and to help. The one place where the Lord's presence and power will be more fully realized than any other place is the closet of prayer.

Paul gives the various terms of prayer, supplication and giving of thanks as the complement of true praying. The soul must be in all of these spiritual exercises. There must be no half-hearted praying, no abridging its nature, and no abating its force, if we would be freed from this undue anxiety which causes friction and internal distress, and if we would receive the rich fruit of that peace which passeth all understanding. He who prays must be an earnest soul, abounding in spiritual attributes.

"In everything, let your requests be made known unto God," says Paul. Nothing is too great to be handled in prayer, or to be sought in prayer. Nothing is too small to be weighed in the secret councils of the closet, and nothing is too little for its final judgment. As care comes from every source, so prayer goes to every source. As there are no small things in prayer, so there are no small things with God. He who counts the hairs of our head, and who is not too lofty and high to notice the little sparrow which falls to the ground, is not too great and high to note everything which concerns the happiness, the needs and the safety of his children. Prayer brings God into what men are pleased to term the little affairs of life. The lives of people are made up of these small matters, and yet how often do great consequences come from small beginnings?

> There is no sorrow, Lord, too light.
> To bring in prayer to thee;
> There is no anxious care too slight
> To wake thy sympathy.
> There is no secret sigh we breathe,
> But meets thine ear divine,
> And every cross grows light beneath
> The shadow, Lord, of thine.

As everything by prayer is to be brought to the notice of Almighty God, so we are assured that whatever affects us concerns him. How comprehensive is this direction about prayer! "In everything by prayer." There is no distinction here between temporal and spiritual things. Such a distinction is against faith, wisdom and reverence. God rules everything in nature and in grace. Man is affected for time and eternity by things secular as well as by things spiritual. Man's salvation hangs on his business as well as on his prayers. A man's business hangs on his prayers just as it hangs on his diligence.

The chief hindrances to piety, the wiliest and the deadliest temptations of the devil, are in business, and lie alongside the things of time. The heaviest, the most confusing and the most stupefying cares lie beside secular and worldly matters. So in everything which comes to us and which concerns us, in everything which we want to come to us, and in everything which we do not want to come to us, prayer is to be made for all. Prayer blesses all things, brings all things, relieves all things, and prevents all things. Everything as well as every place and every hour is to be ordered by prayer. Prayer has in it the possibility to affect everything which affects us. Here are the vast possibilities of prayer.

How much is the bitter of life sweetened by prayer! How are the feeble made strong by prayer! Sickness flees before the health of prayer. Doubts, misgivings, and trembling fears retire before prayer. Wisdom, knowledge, holiness, and heaven are at the command of prayer. Nothing is outside of prayer. It has the power to gain all things in the provision of our Lord Jesus Christ. Paul covers all departments and sweeps the entire field of human concern, conditions, and happenings by saying, "In everything by prayer."

Supplications and thanksgiving are to be joined with prayer. It is not the dignity of worship, the gorgeousness of ceremonials, the magnificence of its ritual, nor the plainness of its sacraments, which avail. It is not simply the soul's hallowed and lowly abasement before God, neither the speechless awe, which benefits in this prayer service, but the intensity of supplication, the looking and the lifting of the soul in ardent plea to God for the things desired and for which request is made.

The radiance and gratitude and utterance of thanksgiving must be there. This is not simply the poetry of praise, but the deep-toned words and the prose of thanks. There must be hearty thanks, which remembers the past, sees God in it, and voices that recognition in sincere thanksgiving. The hidden depths within must have utterance. The lips must speak the music of the soul. A heart enthused of God, a heart illumined by his presence, a life guided by his right hand, must have something to say for God in gratitude. Such is to recognize God in the events of past life, to exalt God for his goodness, and to honor God who has honored it.

"Make known your requests unto God." The "requests" must be made known unto God. Silence is not prayer. Prayer is asking God for something which we have not, which we desire, and which he has promised to give in answer to prayer. Prayer is really verbal asking. Words are in prayer. Strong words and true words are found in prayer. Desires

THE POSSIBILITIES OF PRAYER

in prayer are put in words. The praying one is a pleader. He urges his prayer by arguments, promises, and needs.

Sometimes loud words are in prayer. The psalmist said, "Evening, morning and at noon will I pray, and cry aloud." The praying one wants something which he has not got. He wants something which God has in his possession, and which he can get by praying. He is beggared, bewildered, oppressed, and confused. He is before God in supplication, in prayer, and in thanksgiving. These are the attitudes, the incense, the paraphernalia, and the fashion of this hour, the court attendance of his soul before God.

"Requests" mean to ask for one's self. The man is in a strait. He needs something, and he needs it badly. Other help has failed. It means a plea for something to be given which has not been done. The request is for the giver-not alone his gifts but himself. The requests of the praying one are to be made known unto God. The requests are to be brought to the knowledge of God. It is then that cares fly away, anxieties disappear, worries depart, and the soul gets at ease. Then there steals into the heart "the peace of God that passeth all understanding."

> Peace! doubting heart, my God's I am,
> Who formed me man, forbids my fear;
> The Lord hath called me by my name;
> The Lord protects, forever near;
> His blood for me did once atone,
> And still he loves and guards his own.

In James, chapter five, we have another marvelous description of prayer and its possibilities. It has to do with sickness and health, sin and forgiveness, and rain and drought. Here we have James' directory for praying:

Is any among you afflicted? Let him pray. Is any merry? Let him sing psalms. Is any sick among you? Let him call for the elders of the church, and let them pray over him, anointing him with oil in the name of the Lord. And the prayer of faith shall save the sick; and the Lord shall raise him up; and if he have committed sins, they shall be forgiven him. Confess your faults one to another, and pray one for another, that ye may be healed. The effectual, fervent prayer of a righteous man availeth much. Elijah was a man subject to like passions as we are, and he prayed earnestly that it might not rain, and it rained not on the earth by the space of three years and six months. And he prayed again, and the heaven gave rain, and the earth brought forth her fruit.

Here is prayer for one's own needs and intercessory prayer for others; prayer for physical needs and prayer for spiritual needs; prayer for drought and prayer for rain; prayer for temporal matters and prayer for spiritual things. How vast the reach of prayer! How wonderful under these words its possibilities!

Here is the remedy for affliction and depression of every sort, and here we find the remedy for sickness and for rain in the time of drought. Here is the way to obtain forgiveness of sins. A stroke of prayer paralyzes the energies of nature, stays its clouds, rain and dew, and blasts field and farm like the simoon. Prayer brings clouds, and rain and fertility to the famished and wasted earth.

The general statement, "The effectual, fervent prayer of a righteous man availeth much," is a statement of prayer as an energetic force. Two words are used. One signifies power in exercise, operative power, while the other is power as an endowment. Prayer is power and strength, a power and strength which influences God, and is most salutary, widespread, and marvelous in its gracious benefits to man. Prayer influences God. The ability of God to do for man is the measure of the possibility of prayer.

> Thou art coming to a king,
> Large petitions with thee bring;
> For his grace and power are such
> None can ever ask too much.

10

Answered Prayer

IT is answered prayer which brings praying out of the realm of dry, dead things, and makes praying a thing of life and power. It is the answer to prayer which brings things to pass, changes the natural trend of things, and orders all things according to the will of God. It is the answer to prayer which takes praying out of the regions of fanaticism, and saves it from being Utopian, or from being merely fanciful. It is the answer to prayer which makes praying a power for God and for man, and makes praying real and divine. Unanswered prayers are training schools for unbelief, an imposition and a nuisance, an impertinence to God and to man.

Answers to prayer are the only surety that we have prayed aright. What marvelous power there is in prayer! What untold miracles it works in this world! What untold benefits to men does it secure to those who pray! Why is it that the average prayer by the million goes a begging for an answer?

The millions of unanswered prayers are not to be solved by the mystery of God's will. We are not the sport of his sovereign power. He is not playing at "make-believe" in his marvelous promises to answer prayer. The whole explanation is found in our wrong praying. "We ask and receive not because we ask amiss." If all unanswered prayers were dumped into the ocean, they would come very near filling it. Child of God, can you pray? Are your prayers answered? If not, why not? Answered prayer is the proof of your real praying.

The efficacy of prayer from a Bible standpoint lies solely in the answer to prayer. The benefit of prayer has been well and popularly maximized by the saying, "It moves the arm which moves the universe." To get unquestioned answers to prayer is not only important as to the satisfying of our desires, but is also the evidence of our abiding in Christ. It becomes more important still. The mere act of praying is no test of our relation to God. The act of praying may be a real dead performance. It may be the routine of habit. But to pray and receive clear answers, not once or twice, but daily, this is the sure test, and is the gracious point of our vital connection with Jesus Christ.

Read our Lord's words in this connection: "If ye abide in me, and my words abide in you, ye shall ask what ye will, and it shall be done unto you."

To God and to man, the answer to prayer is the all-important part of our praying. The answer to prayer, direct and unmistakable, is the evidence of God's being. It proves that God lives, that there is a God, an intelligent being, who is interested in his creatures, and who listens to them when they approach him in prayer. There is no proof so clear and demonstrative_ that God exists than prayer and its answer. This was Elijah's plea: "Hear me, O Lord, hear me, that this people may know that thou art the Lord God."

The answer to prayer is the part of prayer which glorifies God. Unanswered prayers are dumb oracles which leave the praying ones in darkness, doubt, and bewilderment, and which carry no conviction to the unbeliever. It is not the act or the attitude of praying which gives efficacy to prayer. It is not abject prostration of the body before God, the vehement or quiet utterance to God, the exquisite beauty and poetry of the diction of our prayers, which do the deed. It is not the marvelous array of argument and eloquence in praying which makes prayer effectual. Not one or all of these are the things which glorify God. It is the answer which brings glory to his name.

Elijah might have prayed on Carmel's heights till this good day with all the fire and energy of his soul, and if no answer had been given, no glory would have come to God. Peter might have shut himself up with Dorcas' dead body till he himself died on his knees, and if no answer had come, no glory to God nor good to man would have followed, but only doubt, blight, and dismay.

Answered prayer is the convincing proof of our right relations to God. Jesus said at the grave of Lazarus:

Father, I thank thee that thou hast heard me. And I knew that thou hearest me always, but because of the people that stand by I said it, that they may believe that thou hast sent me.

The answer of his prayer was the proof of his mission from God, as the answer to Elijah's prayer was made to the woman whose son he raised to life. She said, "Now by this I know that thou art a man of God." He is highest in the favor of God who has the readiest access and the greatest number of answers to prayer from Almighty God.

Prayer ascends to God by an invariable law, even by more than law, by the will, the promise, and the presence of a personal God. The answer comes back to earth by all the promise, the truth, the power, and the love of God.

Not to be concerned about the answer to prayer is not to pray. What a world of waste there is in praying. What myriads of prayers have been offered for which no answer is returned, no answer longed for, and no answer is expected! We have been nurturing a false faith and hiding the shame of our loss and inability to pray, by the false, comforting plea that God does not answer directly or objectively, but indirectly and subjectively. We have persuaded ourselves that by some kind of hocus pocus of which we are wholly unconscious in its process and its results, we have been made better. Conscious that God has not answered us directly, we have solaced ourselves with the delusive unction that God has in some impalpable way, and with unknown results, given us something better. Or we have comforted and nurtured our spiritual sloth by saying that it is not God's will to give it to us. Faith teaches God's praying ones that it is God's will to answer prayer. God answers all prayers and every prayer of his true children who truly pray.

> Prayer makes the darkened cloud withdraw,
> Prayer climbs the ladder Jacob saw;
> Gives exercise to faith and love,
> Brings every blessing from above.

The emphasis in the Scriptures is always given to the answer to prayer. All things from God are given in answer to prayer. God himself, his presence, his gifts and his grace, one and all, are secured by prayer. The medium by which God communicates with men is prayer. The most real thing in prayer, its very essential end, is the answer it secures. The mere repetition of words in prayer, the counting of beads, the multiplying mere words of prayer, as works of supererogation, as if there was virtue in the number of prayers to avail, is a vain delusion, an empty thing, a useless service. Prayer looks directly to securing an answer. This is its design. It has no other end in view.

Communion with God of course is in prayer. There is sweet fellowship there with our God through his Holy Spirit. Enjoyment of God there is in praying, sweet, rich, and strong. The graces of the Spirit in the inner soul are nurtured by prayer, kept alive and promoted in their growth by this spiritual exercise. But not one nor all of these benefits of prayer have in them the essential end of prayer. The divinely appointed channel through which all good and all grace flows to our souls and bodies is prayer.

> Prayer is appointed to convey
> The blessings God designs to give.

Prayer is divinely ordained as the means by which all temporal and spiritual good are gained to us. Prayer is not an end in itself. It is not something done to be rested in, something we have done, about which we are to congratulate ourselves. It is a means to an end. It is something we do which brings us something in return, without which the praying is valueless. Prayer always aims at securing an answer.

We are rich, strong, good, and holy by answered prayer. It is not the mere performance, the attitude, nor the words of prayer, which bring benefit to us, but it is the answer sent direct from heaven. Conscious, real answers to prayer bring real good to us. This is not praying merely for self, or simply for selfish ends. The selfish character cannot exist when the prayer conditions are fulfilled.

It is by these answered prayers that human nature is enriched. The answered prayer brings us into constant and conscious communion with God, awakens and enlarges gratitude, and excites the melody and lofty inspiration of praise. Answered prayer is the mark of God in our praying. It is the exchange with heaven, and it establishes and realizes a relationship with the unseen. We give our prayers in exchange for the divine blessing. God accepts our prayers through the atoning blood and gives himself, his presence, and his grace in return.

All holy affections are affected by answered prayers. By the answers to prayer all holy principles are matured, and faith, love, and hope have their enrichment by answered prayer. The answer is found in all true praying. The answer is in prayer strongly as an aim, a desire expressed, and its expectation and realization give importunity and realization to prayer. It is the fact of the answer which makes the prayer, and which enters into its very being. To seek no answer to prayer takes the desire, the aim, and the heart out of prayer. It makes praying a dead thing, fit only for dumb idols. It is the answer which brings praying into Bible regions, and makes it a desire realized, a pursuit, an interest, that clothes it with flesh and blood, and makes it a prayer, throbbing with all the true life of prayer, affluent with all the paternal relations of giving and receiving, of asking and answering.

God holds all good in his own hands. That good comes to us through our Lord Jesus Christ because of his all atoning merits, by asking it in his name. The only and the sole command in which all the others of its class belong, is "Ask, seek, knock." And the one and sole promise is its counterpart, its necessary equivalent and results: "It shall be given—-ye shall find—-it shall be opened unto you."

God is so much involved in prayer and its hearing and answering, that all of his attributes and his whole being are centered in that great fact. It distinguishes him as peculiarly beneficent, wonderfully good, and powerfully attractive in his nature. " 0 thou that hearest prayer! To thee shall all flesh come."

> Faithful, 0 Lord, thy mercies are
> A rock that cannot move;
> A thousand promises declare
> Thy constancy of love.

Not only does the Word of God stand surety for the answer to prayer, but all the attributes of God conspire to the same end. God's veracity is at stake in the engagements to answer prayer. His wisdom, his truthfulness and his goodness are involved. God's infinite and inflexible rectitude is pledged to the great end of answering the prayers of those who call upon him in time of need. Justice and mercy blend into oneness to secure the answer to prayer. It is significant that the very justice of God comes into play and stands hard by God's faithfulness in the strong promise God makes of the pardon of sins and of cleansing from sin's pollutions:

If we confess our sins, he is faithful and just to forgive us our sins and to cleanse us from all unrighteousness.

God's kingly relation to man, with all of its authority, unites with the fatherly relation and with all of its tenderness to secure the answer to prayer.

Our Lord Jesus Christ is most fully committed to the answer of prayer. "Whatsoever ye shall ask in my name, that will I do, that the Father may be glorified in the Son." How well assured the answer to prayer is, when that answer is to glorify God the Father! And how eager

Jesus Christ is to glorify his Father in heaven! So eager is he to answer prayer which always and everywhere brings glory to the Father, that no prayer offered in his name is denied or overlooked by him. Says our Lord Jesus Christ again, giving fresh assurance to our faith, "If ye shall ask anything in my name, I will do it." So says he once more, "Ask what ye will, and it shall be done unto you."

> Come, my soul, thy suit prepare,
> Jesus loves to answer prayer;
> He himself has bid thee pray,
> Therefore will not say thee nay.

11

Answered Prayer (Continued)

GOD has committed himself to us by his Word in our praying. The Word of God is the basis and the inspiration and the heart of prayer. Jesus Christ stands as the illustration of God's Word, its illimitable good in promise as well as in realization. God takes nothing by halves. He gives nothing by halves. We can have the whole of him when he has the whole of us-His words of promise are so far-reaching, and so all-comprehending, that they seem to have deadened our comprehension and have paralyzed our praying. This appears when we consider those large words, when he almost exhausts human language in promises, as in "whatever," "anything," and in the all-inclusive "whatsoever," and "all things." These oft-repeated promises, so very great, seem to daze us, and instead of allowing them to move us to asking, testing, and receiving, we turn away full of wonder, but empty handed and with empty hearts.

We quote another passage from our Lord's teaching about prayer. By the most solemn verification, he declares as follows:

And in that day ye shall ask me nothing; Verily, Verily, I say unto you: Whatsoever ye shall ask the Father in my name, he will give it to you. Hitherto ye have asked nothing in my name. Ask, and ye shall receive, that your joy may be full.

Twice in this passage he declares the answer, and pledging his father, "He will give it to you," and declaring with impressive and most suggestive emphasis, "Ask, and ye shall receive." So strong and so often did

THE POSSIBILITIES OF PRAYER

Jesus declare and repeat the answer as an inducement to pray, and as an inevitable result of prayer, the apostles held it as so fully and invincibly established, that prayer would be answered, they held it to be their main duty to urge and command men to pray. So firmly were they established as to the truth of the law of prayer as laid down by our Lord, that they were led to affirm that the answer to prayer was involved in and necessarily bound up with all right praying. God the Father and Jesus Christ, his Son, are both strongly committed by all the truth of their word and by the fidelity of their character, to answer prayer.

Not only do these and all the promises pledge Almighty God to answer prayer, but they assure us that the answer will be specific, and that the very thing for which we pray will be given.

Our Lord's invariable teaching was that we receive that for which we ask, and obtain that for which we seek, and have that door opened at which we knock. This is according to our heavenly Father's direction to us, and his giving to us for our asking. He will not disappoint us by not answering, neither will he deny us by giving us some other thing for which we have not asked, or by letting us find some other thing for which we have not sought, or by opening to us the wrong door, at which we were not knocking. If we ask bread, he will give us bread. If we ask an egg, he will give us an egg. If we ask a fish, he will give us a fish. Not something like bread, but bread itself will be given unto us. Not something like a fish, but a fish will be given. Not evil will be given us in answer to prayer, but good.

Earthly parents, though evil in nature, give for the asking, and answer to the crying of their children. The encouragement to prayer is transferred from our earthly father to our heavenly Father, from the evil to the good, to the supremely good; from the weak to the omnipotent, our heavenly Father, centering in himself all the highest conceptions of fatherhood, abler, readier, and much more than the best, and much more than the ablest earthly father. "How much more," who can tell? Much more than our earthly father, will he supply all our needs, give us all good things, and enable us to meet every difficult duty and fulfill every law, though hard to flesh and blood, but made easy under the full supply of our heavenly Father's beneficent and exhaustless help.

Here we have in symbol and as initial, more than an intimation of the necessity, not only of perseverance in prayer, but of the progressive stages of intentness and effort in the outlay of increasing spiritual force. Asking, seeking, and knocking. Here is an ascending scale from the mere words of asking, to a settled attitude of seeking, resulting in a determined, clamorous and vigorous direct effort of praying.

Just as God has commanded us to pray always, to pray everywhere, and to pray in everything, so he will answer always, everywhere and in everything.

God has plainly and with directness committed himself to answer prayer. If we fulfill the conditions of prayer, the answer is bound to come. The laws of nature are not so invariable and so inexorable as the promised answer to pray. The ordinances of nature might fail, but the ordinances of grace can never fail. There are no limitations, no adverse conditions, no weakness, no inability, which can or will hinder the answer to prayer. God's doing for us when we pray has no limitations, is not hedged about, by provisos in himself, or in the peculiar circumstances of any particular case. If we really pray, God masters and defies all things and is above all conditions.

God explicitly says, "Call unto me, and I will answer." There are no limitations, no hedges, no hindrances in the way of God fulfilling the promise. His word is at stake. His word is involved. God solemnly engages to answer prayer. Man is to look for the answer, be inspired by the expectation of the answer, and may with humble boldness demand the answer. God, who cannot lie, is bound to answer. He has voluntarily placed himself under obligation to answer the prayer of him who truly prays.

> To God your every want
> In instant prayer display;
> Pray always; pray, and never faint;

> Pray, without ceasing, pray.
> In fellowship, alone,
> To God with faith draw near;
> Approach his courts, beseech his throne,
> With all the power of prayer.

The prophets and the men of God of Old Testament times were unshaken in their faith in the absolute certainty of God fulfilling his promises to them. They rested in security on the word of God, and had no doubt whatever either as to the fidelity of God in answering prayer or of his willingness or ability. So much so that their history is marked by repeated asking and receiving at the hands of God.

The same is true of the early church. They received without question the doctrine their Lord and Master had so often affirmed that the answer to prayer was sure. The certainty of the answer to prayer was as fixed as God's Word was true. The Holy Spirit dispensation was ushered in by the disciples carrying this faith into practice. When Jesus told them to "Tarry at Jerusalem till they were endued with power from on high," they received it as a sure promise that if they obeyed the command, they would certainly receive the divine power. So in prayer for ten days they tarried in the upper room, and the promise was fulfilled. The answer came just as Jesus said.

So when Peter and John were arrested for healing the man who sat at the beautiful gate of the temple, after being threatened by the rulers in Jerusalem, they were released. "And being let go, they went to their own company," they went to those with whom they were in affinity, those of like minds, and not to men of the world. Still believing in prayer and its power, they gave themselves to prayer, the prayer itself being recorded in Acts, chapter four. They recited some things to the Lord, and "when they had prayed, the place was shaken where they were assembled together, and they were filled with the Holy Spirit, and they spake the word of God with boldness."

Here they were refilled for this special occasion with the Holy Spirit. The answer to prayer responded to their faith and prayer. The fullness of the Spirit always brings boldness. The cure for fear in the face of threatenings of the enemies of the Lord is being filled with the Spirit. This gives power to speak the word of the Lord with boldness. This gives courage and drives away fear.

12

Answered Prayer (Continued)

WE put it to the front. We unfold it on a banner never to be lowered or folded, that God does hear and answer prayer. God has always heard and answered prayer. God will forever hear and answer prayer. He is the same yesterday, today and forever, ever blessed, ever to be adored. Amen. He changes not. As he has always answered prayer, so will he ever continue to do so.

To answer prayer is God's universal rule. It is his unchangeable and irrepealable law to answer prayer. It is his invariable, specific and inviolate promise to answer prayer. The few denials to prayer in the Scriptures are the exceptions to the general rule, suggestive and startling by their fewness, exception and emphasis.

The possibilities of prayer, then, lie in the great truth, illimitable in its broadness, fathomless in its depths, exhaustless in its fullness, that God answers every prayer from every true soul who truly prays.

God's Word does not say, "Call unto me, and you will thereby be trained into the happy art of knowing how to be denied. Ask, and you will learn sweet patience by getting nothing." Far from it. But it is definite, clear and positive: "Ask, and it shall be given unto you."

We have this case among many in the Old Testament:

Jabez called on the God of Israel, saying, 0 that thou wouldst bless me indeed, and enlarge my coast, and that thy hand might be with me, and that thou wouldst keep me from evil, that it may not grieve me.

And God readily granted him the things which he had requested.

Hannah, distressed in soul because she was childless, and desiring a man child, repaired to the house of prayer, and prayed, and this is the record she makes of the direct answer she received: "For this child I prayed, and the Lord hath given me the petition which I asked of him."

God's promises and purposes go direct to the fact of giving for the asking. The answer to our prayers is the motive constantly presented in the Scriptures to encourage us to pray and to quicken us in this spiritual exercise. Take such strong, clear passages as these:

Call unto me, and I will answer thee. He shall call unto me, and I will answer. Ask, and it shall be given you. Seek, and ye shall find. Knock, and it shall be opened unto you.

This is Jesus Christ's law of prayer. He does not say, "Ask, and something shall be given you." Nor does he say, "Ask, and you will be trained into piety." But it is that when you ask, the very thing asked for will be given. Jesus does not say, "Knock, and some door will be opened." But the very door at which you are knocking will be opened. To make this doubly sure, Jesus Christ duplicates and reiterates the promise of the answer: "For every one that asketh, receiveth; and he that seeketh, findeth; and to him that knocketh, it shall be opened."

Answered prayer is the spring of love, and is the direct encouragement to pray. "I love the Lord because he hath heard my voice and my supplications. Because he hath inclined his ear unto me, therefore will I call upon him as long as I live."

The certainty of the father's giving is assured by the father's relation, and by the ability and goodness of the father. Earthly parents, frail, infirm, and limited in goodness and ability, give when the child asks and seeks. The parental heart responds most readily to the cry for bread. The hunger of the child touches and wins the father heart. So God, our heavenly Father, is as easily and strongly moved by our prayers as the earthly parent. "If ye being evil, know how to give good gifts unto your children, how much more shall your Father in heaven give good gifts unto them that ask him?" "Much more," just as much more does God's goodness, tenderness and ability exceed that of man's.

Just as the asking is specific, so also is the answer specific. The child does not ask for one thing and get another. He does not cry for bread, and get a stone. He does not ask for an egg, and receive a scorpion. He does not ask for a fish, and get a serpent. Christ demands specific asking. He responds to specific praying by specific giving.

To give the very thing prayed for, and not something else, is fundamental to Christ's law of praying. No prayer for the cure of blind eyes did he ever answer by curing deaf ears. The very thing prayed for is the very thing which he gives. The exceptions to this are confirmatory of this great law of prayer. He who asks for bread gets bread, and not a stone. If he asks for a fish, he receives a fish, and not a serpent. No cry is so pleading and so powerful as the child's cry for bread. The cravings of hunger, the appetite felt, and the need realized, all create and propel the crying of the child. Our prayers must be as earnest, as needy, and as hungry as the hungry child's cry for bread. Simple, artless, direct, and specific must be our praying, according to Christ's law of prayer and his teaching of God's fatherhood.

The illustration and enforcement of the law of prayer are found in the specific answers given to prayer. Gethsemane is the only seeming exception. The prayer of Jesus Christ in that awful hour of darkness and hell was conditioned on these words, "If it be possible, let this cup pass from me." But beyond these utterances of our Lord was the soul and life prayer of the willing, suffering divine victim, "Nevertheless not as I will, but as thou wilt." The prayer was answered, the angel came, strength was imparted, and the meek sufferer in silence drank the bitter cup.

Two cases of unanswered prayer are recorded in the Scriptures in addition to the Gethsemane prayer of our Lord. The first was that of David for the life of his baby child, but for good reasons to Almighty God the request was not granted. The second was that of Paul for the removal of the thorn in the flesh, which was denied. But we are constrained to believe these must have been notable as exceptions to God's rule, as illustrated in the history of prophet, priest, apostle and saint, as recorded in the divine Word. There must have been unrevealed reasons which moved God to veer from his settled and fixed rule to answer prayer by giving the specific thing prayed for.

Our Lord did not hold the Syrophoenician woman in the school of unanswered prayer to test and mature her faith, neither did he answer her prayer by healing or saving her husband. She asks for the healing of her daughter, and Christ healed the daughter. She received the very thing for which she asked the Lord Jesus Christ. It was in the school of answered prayer our Lord disciplined and perfected her faith, and it was by giving her a specific answer to her prayer. Her prayer centered on her daughter. She prayed for the one thing, the healing of her child. And the answer of our Lord centered likewise on the daughter.

We tread altogether too gingerly upon the great and precious promises of God, and too often we ignore them wholly. The promise is the ground on which faith stands in asking of God. This is the one basis of prayer. We limit God's ability. We measure God's ability and willingness to answer prayer by the standard of men. We limit the Holy One of Israel. How full of benefaction and remedy to suffering mankind are the promises as given us by James in his Epistle, fifth chapter! How personal and mediate do they make God in prayer! They are a direct challenge to our faith. They are encouraging to large expectations in all the requests we make of God. Prayer affects God in a direct manner, and has its aim and end inaffecting him. Prayer takes hold of God, and induces him to do large things for us, whether personal or relative, temporal or spiritual, earthly or heavenly.

The great gap between Bible promises to prayer and the income from praying is almost unspeakably great, so much so that it is a prolific source of infidelity. It breeds unbelief in prayer as a great moral force, and begets doubt really as to the power of prayer. Christianity needs today, above all things else, men and women who can in prayer put God to the test and who can prove his promises. When this happy day for the world begins, it will be earth's brightest day, and will be heaven's dawning day on earth. These are the sort of men and women needed in this modern day in the church. It is not educated men who are needed for the times. It is not more money that is required. It is not more machinery, more organization, more ecclesiastical laws, but it is men and women who know how to pray, who can in prayer lay hold upon God and bring him down to earth, and move him to take hold of earth's affairs mightily and put life and power into the church and into all of its machinery.

The church and the world greatly need saints who can bridge this wide gap between the praying done and the small number of answers received. Saints are needed whose faith is bold enough and sufficiently far-reaching to put God to the test. The cry comes even now out of heaven to the people of the present-day church, as it sounded forth in the days of Malachi: "Prove me now herewith, saith the Lord of hosts." God is waiting to be put to the test by his people in prayer. He delights in being put to the test on his promises. It is his highest pleasure to answer prayer to prove the reliability of his promises. Nothing worthy of God nor of great value to men will be accomplished till this is done.

Our gospel belongs to the miraculous. It was projected on the miraculous plane. It cannot be maintained but by the supernatural. Take the supernatural out of our holy religion, and its life and power are gone, and it degenerates into a mere mode of morals. The miraculous is divine power. Prayer has in it this same power. Prayer brings this divine power into the ranks of men and puts it to work. Prayer brings into the affairs of earth a supernatural element. Our gospel when truly presented is the power of God. Never was the church more in need of those who can and will test Almighty God. Never did the church need more than now those who can raise up everywhere memorials of God's supernatural power, memorials of answers to prayer, memorials of promises fulfilled. These would do more to silence the enemy of souls, the foe of God and the adversary of the church than any modern scheme or present day plan for the success of the gospel. Such memorials reared by praying people would dumbfound God's foes, strengthen weak saints, and would fill strong saints with triumphant rapture.

The most prolific source of infidelity, and that which maligns and hinders praying, and that which obscures the being and glory of God most effectually, is unanswered prayer. Better not to pray at all than to go through a dead form, which secures no answer, brings no glory to God, and supplies no good to man. Nothing so hardens the heart and nothing so blinds us to the unseen and the eternal, as this kind of prayerless praying.

13

Prayer Miracles

THE earthly career of our Lord Jesus Christ was no mere episode, a sort of interlude, in his eternal life. What he was and what he did on earth was neither abnormal nor divergent, but characteristic. What he was and what he did on earth is but the figure and the illustration of what he is and what he is doing in heaven. He is "the same yesterday and today, and forever." This statement is the divine summary of the eternal unity and changelessness of his character. His earthly life was made up largely of hearing and answering prayer. His heavenly life is devoted to the same divine business. Really the Old Testament is the record of God hearing and answering prayer. The whole Bible deals largely with this all important subject.

Christ's miracles are object lessons. They are living pictures. They talk to us. They have hands which take hold of us. Many valuable lessons do these miracles teach us. In their diversity, they refresh us. They show us the matchless power of Jesus Christ, and at the same time discover to us his marvelous compassion for suffering humanity. These miracles disclose to us his ability to endlessly diversify his operations. God's method in working with man is not the same in all cases. He does not administer his grace in rigid ruts. There is endless variety in his movements. There is marvelous diversity in his operations. He does not fashion his creations in the same mold. Just so our Lord is not circumscribed in his working nor trammeled by models. He works independently. He is his own architect. He furnishes his own patterns which have unlimited variety.

When we consider our Lord's miracles, we discover that quite a number were performed unconditionally. At least there were no conditions accompanying them so far as the divine record shows. At his own instance, without being solicited to do so, to glorify God and to manifest his own glory and power, this class of miracles was wrought. Many of his mighty works were performed at the moving of his compassion and at the call of suffering and need, as well as at the call of his power. But a number of them were performed by him in answer to prayer. Some were wrought in answer to the personal prayers of those who were afflicted. Others were performed in answer to the prayers of the friends of those who were afflicted. Those miracles wrought in answer to prayer are very instructive in the uses of prayer. In these conditional miracles, faith holds the primacy and prayer is faith's deputy. We have an illustration of the importance of faith as the condition on which the exercise of Christ's power was based, or the channel through which it flowed, in the incident of a visit he made to Nazareth with its results, or rather its lack of results. Here is the record of the case:

And he could there do no mighty work, save that he laid his hands upon a few sick folk, and healed them. And he marvelled because of their unbelief.

Those people at Nazareth may have prayed our Lord to raise their dead, or open the eyes of the blind, or heal the lepers, but it was all in vain. The absence of faith, however much of performance may be seen, restrains the exercise of God's power, paralyzes the arm of Christ, and turns to death all signs of life : Unbelief is the one thing which seriously hinders Almighty God in doing mighty works. Matthew's record of this visit to Nazareth says, "And he did not any mighty works there because of their unbelief." Lack of faith ties the hands of Almighty God in his working among the children of men. Prayer to Christ must always be based, backed, and impregnated with faith.

THE POSSIBILITIES OF PRAYER

The miracle of miracles in the earthly career of our Lord, the raising of Lazarus from the dead, was remarkable for its prayer accompaniment. It was really a prayer issue, something after the issue between the prophets of Baal and Elijah. It was not a prayer for help. It was one of thanksgiving and assured confidence. Let us read it:

And Jesus lifted up his eyes and said, Father, I thank thee that thou hast heard me. And I know that thou hearest me always. But because of the people that stand by, I said it, that they may believe that thou hast sent me.

It was a prayer mainly for the benefit of those who were present, that they might know that God was with him because he had answered his prayers, and that faith in God might be radiated in their hearts.

Answered prayers are sometimes the most convincing and faith-creating forces. Unanswered prayers chill the atmosphere and freeze the soil of faith. If Christians knew how to pray so as to have answers to their prayers, evident, immediate, and demonstrative answers from God, faith would be more widely diffused, would become more general, would be more profound, and would be a much more mighty force in the world.

What a valuable lesson of faith and intercessory prayer does the miracle of the healing of the centurion's servant bring to us! The simplicity and strength of the faith of this Roman officer are remarkable, for he believed that it was not needful for our Lord to go directly to his house to have his request granted, "But speak the word only, and my servant shall be healed." And our Lord puts his mark upon this man's faith by saying, "Verily I say unto you, I have not found so great faith, no, not in Israel." This man's prayer was the expression of his strong faith, and such faith brought the answer promptly.

The same invaluable lesson we get from the prayer miracle of the case of the Syrophoenician woman who went to our Lord in behalf of her stricken daughter, making her daughter's case her own, by pleading, "Lord, help me." Here was importunity, holding on, pressing her case, refusing to let go or to be denied. A strong case it was of intercessory prayer and its benefits. Our Lord seemingly held her off for a while but at last yielded, and put his seal upon her strong faith: "O woman, great is thy faith! Be it unto thee even as thou wilt." What a lesson on praying for others and its large benefits!

Individual cases could be named, where the afflicted persons interceded for themselves, illustrations of wonderful things wrought by our Lord in answer to the cries of those who were afflicted. As we read the evangelists' record, the pages fairly glisten with records of our Lord's miracles wrought in answer to prayer, showing the wonderful things accomplished by the use of this divinely appointed means of grace.

If we turn back to Old Testament times, we have no lack of instances of prayer miracles. The saints of those days were well acquainted with the power of prayer to move God to do great things. Natural laws did not stand in the way of Almighty God when he was appealed to by his praying ones. What a marvelous record is that of Moses as those successive plagues were visited upon Egypt in the effort to make Pharaoh let the children of Israel go that they might serve God! As one after another of these plagues came, Pharaoh would beseech Moses, "Entreat the Lord your God that he may take away this death." And as the plagues themselves were miracles, prayer removed them as quickly as they were sent by Almighty God. The same hand which sent these destructive agencies upon Egypt was moved by the prayers of his servant Moses to remove these same plagues. And the removal of the plagues in answer to prayer was as remarkable a display of divine power as was the sending of the plagues in the first instance. The removal in answer to prayer would do as much to show God's being and his power as would the plagues themselves. They were miracles of prayer.

All down the line in Old Testament days we see these prayer miracles. God's praying servants had not the least doubt that prayer would work marvelous results and bring the supernatural into the affairs of earth. Miracles and prayer went hand in hand. They were companions. The one was the cause, the other was the effect. The one brought the other into existence. The miracle was the proof that God heard and answered prayer. The miracle was the divine demonstration that God, who was in heaven, interfered in earth's affairs, intervened to help men, and worked supernaturally if need be to accomplish his purposes in answer to prayer.

Passing to the days of the early church, we find the same divine record of prayer miracles. The sad news came to Peter that Dorcas was dead and he was wanted at Joppa. Promptly he made his way to that place. Peter put everybody out of the room, and then he kneeled down and prayed, and with faith said, "Tabitha, arise," and she opened her eyes and sat up. Knee work on the part of Peter did the work. Prayer brought things to pass and saved Dorcas for further work on earth.

Paul was on that noted journey to Rome under guard, and had been shipwrecked on an island. The chief man of the island was Publius, and his old father was critically ill of a bloody flux. Paul laid his hands on the old man, and prayed for him, and God came to the rescue and healed the sick man. Prayer brought the thing desired to pass. God interfered with the laws of nature, either suspending or setting them aside for a season, and answered the prayer of this praying servant of his. And the answer to prayer among those heathen people convinced them that a supernatural power was at work among them. In fact so true was this that they seemed to think a supernatural being had come among them.

After Herod killed James with the sword, Herod had Peter put in prison. The young church was greatly concerned, but they neither lost heart nor gave themselves over to needless fretting and worrying. They had learned before this from whence their help came. They had been schooled in the lesson of prayer. God had intervened before in the behalf of his servants and interfered when his cause was at stake. "Prayer was made without ceasing of the church unto God for him." An angel on swift wings comes to the rescue, and in a marvelous and supernatural way releases Peter and leaves the prison doors locked. Locks and prison doors and an unfriendly king cannot stand in the way of Almighty God when his people cry in prayer unto him. Miracles if need be will be wrought in their behalf to fulfill his promises and to carry forward his plans. After this order does the Word of God illustrate and enlarge and confirm the possibilities of prayer by what may be termed "Prayer miracles."

How quickly to our straits follow our enlargements! God wrought a wonderful work through Samson in enabling him with a crude instrument, the jawbone of an ass, to slay a thousand men, giving him a great deliverance. Shortly afterward Samson was abnormally thirsty, and he was unable to obtain any water. It seemed as if he would perish with thirst. God had saved him from the hands of the Philistines. Could he not as well save him from thirst? "So Samson cried unto the Lord, and God clave a hollow place that was in the jaw, and there came water thereout, and when he had drunk, his spirit came again and he revived." God could bring water out of the jawbone just as well as he could give victory by it to Samson. God could change that which had been death-dealing to his enemies and make it life-giving to his servant. God can and will work a miracle in answer to prayer to deliver his friends, sooner than he will work one to destroy his enemies. He does both, however, in answer to prayer.

All natural forces are under God's control. He did not create the world and put it under law, and then retire from it, to work out its own destiny, irrespective of the welfare of his intelligent creatures. Natural laws are simply God's laws, by which he governs and regulates all things in nature. Nature is nothing but God's servant. God is above nature, God is not the slave of nature. This being true, God can and will suspend the working of nature's laws, can hold them in abeyance by his almighty hand, can for the time being set them aside, to fulfill his higher purposes in redemption. It is no violation of nature's laws when, in answer to prayer, he who is above nature makes nature his servant, and causes nature to carry out his plans and purposes.

This is the explanation of that wonderful prayer miracle of Old Testament times, when Joshua, in the strength and power of the Lord God, commanded the sun and moon to stand still to give time to complete the victory over the enemies of Israel. Why should it be thought a thing incredible that the God of nature and of grace should interfere with his own natural laws for a short season in answer to prayer, and for the good of his cause? Is God tied hand and foot? Has he so circumscribed himself that he cannot operate the law of prayer? Is the law of nature superior to the law of prayer? Not by any means. He is the God of prayer as well as the God of nature. Both prayer and nature have God as their maker, their ruler and their executor. And prayer is God's servant, just as nature is his servant.

The prayer force in God's government is as strong as any other force, and all natural and other forces must give way before the force of prayer. Sun, moon and stars are under God's control in answer to prayer. Rain, sunshine and drought obey his will. "Fire and hail, snow and vapor, stormy wind fulfilling his word." Disease and health are governed by him. All, all things in heaven and earth, are absolutely under the control of him who made heaven and earth, and who governs all things according to his own will.

Prayer still works miracles among men and brings to pass great things. It is as true now as when James wrote his epistle, "The effectual fervent, prayer of a righteous man availeth much." And when the records of eternity are read out to an assembled world, then will it appear how much prayer has wrought in this world. Little is now seen of the fruits of prayer compared to all that it has accomplished and is accomplishing. At the judgment day, then will God disclose the things which were brought to pass in this world through the prayers of the saints. Many occurrences which are now taken as a matter of course will then be seen to have happened because of the Lord's praying ones.

The work of George Muller in Bristol, England, was a miracle of the nineteenth century. It will take the opening of the books at the great judgment day to disclose all he wrought through prayer. This godly man never asked anyone for money for running expenses at his orphanage where hundreds of fatherless and motherless children were cared for. His practice was always to ask God for just what was needed, and the answers which came to him read like a record of apostolic times.

He prayed for everything and trusted implicitly to God to supply all his needs. And it is a matter of record that never did he and the orphans ever lack for any good thing.

Of a holy man who has done so much for Christ and suffering humanity, it was said at the grave about him:

He prayed up the walls of an hospital, and the hearts of the nurses. He prayed mission stations into being, and missionaries into faith. He prayed open the hearts of the rich, and gold from the most distant lands.

Luther is quoted as once saying: "The Christian's trade is praying." Certainly, for a great reason, the preacher's trade should be praying. We fear greatly that many preachers know nothing of this trade of praying, and hence they never succeed at this trade. A severe apprenticeship in the trade of praying must be served in order to become a journeyman in it. Not only is it true that there are few journeymen at work at this praying trade, but many have never even been apprentices at praying. No wonder so little is accomplished by them. God and the supernatural are left out of their programs.

Many do not understand this trade of praying because they have never learned it, and hence do not work at it. Many miracles ought to be worked by our praying. Why not? Is the arm of the Lord shortened that he cannot save? Is his ear heavy that he cannot hear? Has prayer lost its power because iniquity abounds and the love of many has grown cold? Has God changed from what he once was? To all these queries we enter an emphatic negative. God can as easily today work miracles by praying as he did in the days of old. "I am the Lord; I change not." "Is anything too hard for the Lord?"

He who works miracles by praying will first of all work the chief miracle on himself. Oh, that we might fully understand well the Christian's trade of praying, and follow the trade day by day and thus make for ourselves great spiritual wealth!

14

Wonders of God Through Prayer

In the fearful contest in this world between God and the devil, between good and evil, and between heaven and hell, prayer is the mighty force for overcoming Satan, giving dominion over sin, and defeating hell. Only praying leaders are to be counted on in this dreadful conflict. Praying men alone are to be put to the front. These are the only sort who are able to successfully contend with all the evil forces.

The prayers of all saints are a perpetual force against all the powers of darkness. These prayers are a mighty energy in overcoming the world, the flesh and the devil, and in shaping the destiny of God's movements, to overcome evil and get the victory over the devil and all his works. The character and energy of God's movements lie in prayer. Victory is to come at the end of praying.

The wonders of God's power are to be kept alive, made real and present, and repeated only by prayer. God is not now so evident in the world, so almighty in manifestation as of old, not because miracles have passed away, nor because God has ceased to work, but because prayer has been shorn of its simplicity, its majesty, and its power. God still lives, and miracles still live while God lives and acts, for miracles are God's ways of acting. Prayer is dwarfed, withered, and petrified when faith in God is staggered by doubts of lies ability, or through the shrinking caused by fear. When faith has a telescopic far-off vision of God, prayer works no miracles, and brings no marvels of deliverance. But when God is seen by faith's closest, fullest eye, prayer makes a history of wonders.

Think about God. Make much of him, till he broadens and fills the horizon d faith. Then prayer will come into its marvelous inheritance of wonders. The marvels of prayer are seen when we remember that God's purposes are changed by prayer, God's vengeance is stayed by prayer, and God's penalty is remitted by prayer. The whole range of God's dealing with man is affected by prayer. Here is a force which must be increasingly used, that of prayer, a force which all the events of life ought to be subjected.

To "pray without ceasing," to pray in everything, and to pray everywhere—these commands of continuity are expressive of the sleepless energy of prayer, of the exhaustless possibilities of prayer, and of its exacting necessity. Prayer can do all things. Prayer must do all things.

> Prayer is the simplest form of speech
> That infant lips can try;
> Prayer the sublimest strains that reach
> The majesty on high.

Prayer is asking God for something, and for something which he has promised. Prayer is using the divinely appointed means for obtaining what we need and for accomplishing what God proposes to do on earth.

> Prayer is appointed to convey
> The blessings God designs to give;
> Long as they live should Christians pray,
> They learn to pray when first they live.

And prayer brings to us blessings which we need, and which only God can give, and which prayer can alone convey to us.

In their broadest fullness, the possibilities of prayer are to be found in the very nature of prayer. This service of prayer is not a mere rite, a ceremony through which we go, a sort of performance. Prayer is going to God for something needed and desired. Prayer is simply asking God to do for us what he has promised us he will do if we ask him. The answer is a part of prayer, and is God's part of it. God's doing the thing asked for is as much a part of the prayer as the asking of the thing is prayer. Asking is man's part. Giving is God's part. The praying belongs to us. The answer belongs to God.

Man makes the plea and God makes the answer. The plea and the answer compose the prayer. God is more ready, more willing and more anxious to give the answer than man is to give the asking. The possibilities of prayer lie in the ability of man to ask large things and in the ability of God to give large things.

God's only condition and limitation of prayer is found in the character of the one who prays. The measure of our faith and praying is the measure of his giving. As our Lord said to the blind man, "according to your faith be it unto you," so it is the same in praying, "According to the measure of your asking, be it unto you." God measures the answer according to the prayer. He is limited by the law of prayer in the measure of the answers he gives to prayer. As is the measure of prayer, so will be the answer.

If the person praying has the characteristics which warrant praying, then the possibilities are unlimited. They are declared to be "all things whatsoever." Here is no limitation in character or kind, in circumference or condition. The man who prays can pray for anything and for everything, and God will give everything and anything. If we limit God in the asking, he will be limited in the giving.

Looking ahead, God declares in his Word that the wonder of wonders will be so great in the last days that everything animate and inanimate will be excited by his power:

For behold, I create new heavens and a new earth; and the former shall not be remembered nor come to mind. But be ye glad and rejoice, forever, in that which I create; for behold I create Jerusalem a rejoicing, and her people a joy.

But these days of God's mighty working, the days of his magnificent and wonder-creating power, will be days of magnificent praying.

And it shall come to pass that before they call, I will answer, and while they are yet speaking, I will hear.

It has ever been so. God's marvelous, miracle-working times have been times of marvelous, miracle-working praying. The greatest thing in God's worship by his own estimate is praying. Its chief service and its distinguishing feature is prayer:

Even them will I bring to my holy mountain, and make them joyful in my house of prayer; their burnt offering and their sacrifices shall be accepted upon my altar, for my house shall be called a house of prayer for all people.

This was true under all the gorgeous rites and parade of ceremonies under the Jewish worship. Sacrifice, offering, and the atoning blood were all to be impregnated with prayer. The smoke of burnt offering and perfumed incense which filled God's house was to be but the flame of prayer, and all of God's people were to be anointed priests to minister at his altar of prayer. So all things were to be done with mighty prayer, because mighty prayer was the fruitage and inspiration of mighty faith. But much more is it now true every way under the more simple service of the gospel.

The course of nature, the movements of the planets, and the clouds, have yielded to the influence of prayer, and God has changed and checked the order of the sun and the seasons under the mighty energies of prayer. It is only necessary to note the remarkable incident when Joshua, through this divine means of prayer, caused the sun and the moon to stand still so that a more complete victory could be given to the armies of Israel in the contest with the armies of the Amorites.

If we believe God's Word, we are bound to believe that prayer affects God, and affects him mightily; that prayer avails, and that prayer avails mightily. There are wonders in prayer because there are wonders in God. Prayer has no talismanic influence. It is no mere fetish. It has no so-called powers of magic. It is simply making known our requests to

THE POSSIBILITIES OF PRAYER

God for things agreeable to his will in the name of Christ. It is just yielding our requests to a father, who knows all things, who has control of all things, and who is able to do all things. Prayer is infinite ignorance trusting to the wisdom of God. Prayer is the voice of need crying out to him who is inexhaustible in resources. Prayer is helplessness reposing with childlike confidence on the word of its Father in heaven. Prayer is but the verbal expression of the heart of perfect confidence in the infinite wisdom, the power and the riches of Almighty God, who has placed at our command in prayer everything we need.

How all the gracious results of such gracious times are to come to the world through prayer, we are taught in God's Word. God's heart seems to overflow with delight at the prospect of thus blessing his people. By the mouth of the prophet Joel, God thus speaks:

Fear not, 0 land; be glad and rejoice; for the Lord will do great things." Be not afraid, ye beasts of the field; for the pastures of the wilderness do spring, for the tree beareth her fruit, the fig-tree and the vine do yield their strength. Be glad then, ye children of Zion, and rejoice in the Lord your God; for he hath given you the former rain moderately, and he will cause to come down for you the rain, the former rain, and the latter rain in the first month. And the floors shall be full of wheat, and the vats shall overflow with wine and oil. And I will restore to you the years that the locust hath eaten, the canker worm and the caterpillar, and the palmer worm, my great army which I sent among you. And ye shall eat in plenty, and be satisfied, and praise the name of the Lord your God, that hath dealt wondrously with you; and my people shall never be ashamed. And ye shall know that I am in the midst of Israel, and that I am the Lord your God, and none else; and my people shall never be ashamed.

What wonderful material things are these which God proposes to bestow upon his people! They are marvelous temporal blessings he promises to bestow on them. They almost astonish the mind when they are studied. But God does not restrict his large blessings to temporal things. Looking down the ages, he foresees Pentecost, and makes these exceeding great and precious promises concerning the outpouring of the Holy Spirit, these very words being quoted by Peter on that glad day of Pentecost:

And it shall come to pass afterward, that I will pour out my Spirit upon all flesh; and your sons shall prophesy, your old men shall dream dreams, your young men shall see visions; And also upon the servants and upon the hand maidens in those days will I pour out my Spirit. And I will show wonders in the heavens and in the earth, blood, and fire, and pillars of smoke; The sun shall be turned into darkness, and the moon into blood, before the great and the terrible day of the Lord shall come. And it shall come to pass that whosoever shall call on the name of the Lord shall be delivered; for in Mount Zion and in Jerusalem shall be deliverance, as the Lord hath said, and in the remnant whom the Lord shall call.

But these marvelous blessings will not be bestowed upon the people h. sovereign power, nor be given unconditionally. God's people must do something precedent to such glorious results. Fasting and prayer must play an important part as conditions of receiving such large blessings. By the mouth of the same prophet, God thus speaks:

Therefore also now, saith the Lord, turn ye to me with all your heart, and with fasting, and with weeping, and with mourning; And rend your heart, and not your garments; and turn unto the Lord your God; for he is gracious and merciful, slow to anger, and of great kindness, and repenteth him of the evil. Who knoweth if he will turn and repent, and leave a blessing behind him, even a meat offering, and a drink offering, unto the Lord your God? Blow the trumpet in Zion; sanctify a fast, call a solemn assembly. Gather the people; sanctify the congregation; assemble the elders; gather the children; and those that suck the breasts; let the bridegroom go forth of his chamber, and the bride out of her closet. Let the priests, the ministers of the Lord, weep between the porch and the altar, and let them say, Spare thy people, 0 Lord, and give not thine heritage to reproach, that the heathen should rule over them; Wherefore should they say among the people, Where is their God? Then will

THE POSSIBILITIES OF PRAYER

the Lord be jealous for his land, and pity his people. Yea, the Lord will answer and say unto his people, Behold I will send you corn, and wine, and oil, and ye shall be satisfied therewith; and I will no more make you a reproach among the heathen."

Prayer reaches even as far as the presence of God goes. It reaches everywhere because God is everywhere. Let us read from Psalm 139:1:

If I ascend up into heaven, thou art there; if I make my bed in hell, behold thou art there. If I take the wings of the morning and dwell in the uttermost part of the sea; Even there shall thy hand lead me, and thy right hand shall hold me."

This may be said as truly of prayer as it is said of the God of prayer. The mysteries of death have been fathomed by prayer, and its victims have been brought back to life by the power of prayer, because God holds dominion over death, and prayer reaches where God reigns. Elisha and Elijah both invaded the realms of death by their prayers, and asserted and established the power of God as the power of prayer. Peter by prayer brings back to life the saintly Dorcas to the early church. Paul doubtless exercised the power of prayer as he fell upon and embraced Eutychus who fell out of the window when Paul preached at night.

Our Lord several times explicitly declared the far-reaching possibilities and the unlimited nature of prayer as covering "all things whatsoever." The conditions of prayer are exalted into a personal union with himself. That successful praying glorified God was the condition upon which laborers of first quality and sufficient in numbers were to be secured to press forward God's work in the world. The giving of all good things is conditioned upon asking for them. The giving of the Holy Spirit to God's children is based upon the asking of the children of God. God's will on earth can be secured only by prayer. Daily bread is obtained and sanctified by prayer. Reverence, forgiveness of sins, and deliverance from the evil one, and salvation from temptation, are in the hands of prayer.

The first jeweled foundation Christ lays as the basic principle of his religion in the Sermon on the Mount reads on this wise: "Blessed are the poor in spirit, for theirs is the kingdom of heaven." As prayer follows from the inner sense of need, and prayer is the utterance of a deep poverty-stricken spirit, so it is evident he who is "poor in spirit" is where he can pray and where he does pray.

Prayer is a tremendous force in the world. Take this picture of prayer and its wonderful possibilities. God's cause is quiet and motionless on the earth. An angel, strong and impatient to be of service, waits round about the throne of God in heaven, and to move things on earth and give impetus to the movements of God's cause in this world, he gathers all the prayers of all God's saints in all ages, and puts them before God just like Aaron used to cloud, flavor, and sweeten himself with the delicious incense when he entered the holy sanctuary, made aweful by the immediate presence of God. The angel impregnates all the air with that holy offering of prayers, and then takes its fiery body and casts it on the earth.

Note the remarkable result. "There were voices and thunderings and lightnings and an earthquake." What tremendous force is this which has thus convulsed the earth? The answer is that it is the "prayers of the saints," turned loose by the angel round about the throne, who has charge of those prayers. This mighty force is prayer, like the power of earth's mightiest dynamite.

Take another fact showing the wonders of prayer wrought by Almighty God in answer to the praying of his true prophet. The nation of God's people was fearfully apostate in head and heart and life. A man of God went to the apostate king with the fearful message which meant so much to the land, "There shall not be rain nor dew these years but according to my word." Whence this mighty force which can stay the clouds, seal up the rain, and hold back the dew? Who is this who speaks with such authority? Is there any force which can do this on earth? Only one, and that force is prayer, wielded in the hands of a praying prophet of God. It is he who has influence with God and over God in prayer, who thus dares to assume such authority over the forces of nature. This man Elijah is skilled in the use of that tremendous force. "And Elijah prayed earnestly, and it rained not on the earth for three years and six months."

But this is not all the story. He who could by prayer lock up the clouds and seal up the rain, could also unlock the clouds and unseal the rain by the same mighty power of prayer. "And he prayed again, and the heaven gave rain, and the earth gave forth her fruit."

Mighty is the power of prayer. Wonderful are its fruits. Remarkable things are brought to pass by men of prayer. Many are the wonders of prayer wrought by an almighty hand. The evidences of prayer's accomplishments almost stagger us. They challenge our faith. They encourage our expectations when we pray.

From a cursory summary like this, we get a bird's-eye view of the large possibilities of prayer and the urgent necessity of prayer. We see how God commits himself into the hands of those who truly pray. Great are the wonders of prayer because great is the God who hears and answers prayer. Great are these wonders because great are the rich promises made by a great God to those who pray.

We have seen prayer's far-reaching possibilities and its absolute, unquestioned necessity, and we have also seen that the foregoing particulars and elaboration were requisite in order to bring the subject more clearly, truly and strongly before our minds. The church more than ever needs profound convictions of the vast importance of prayer in prosecuting the work committed to it. More praying must be done and better praying if the church shall be able to perform the difficult, delicate, and responsible task given to it by her Lord and master. Defeat awaits a nonpraying church. Success is sure to follow a church given to much prayer. The supernatural element in the church, without which it must fail, comes only through praying. More time, in this busy bustling age, must be given to prayer by a God-called church. More thought must be given to prayer in this thoughtless, silly age of superficial religion. More heart and soul must be in the praying that is done if the church would go forth in the strength of her Lord and perform the wonders which is her heritage by divine promise.

> O Spirit of the living God,
> In all thy plenitude of grace,
> Where'er the foot of man hath trod,
> Descend on our apostate race.
> Give tongues of fire and hearts of love,
> To preach the reconciling word,
> Give power and unction from above,
> Where'er the joyful sound is heard.

It might be in order to give an instance or two in the life of Rev. John Wesley, showing some remarkable displays of spiritual power. Many times it is stated this noted man gathered his company together, and prayed all night, or till the mighty power of God came upon them. It was at a watch night service, at Fetter Lane, December 31, 1738, when Charles and John Wesley, with Whitfield, sat up till after midnight singing and praying. This is the account:

About three o'clock in the morning, as we were continuing instant in prayer, the power of God came mightily upon us, so that many cried out for exceeding joy, and many fell to the ground. As soon as we had recovered a little from that awe and amazement at the presence of his majesty, we broke out with one voice,

"We praise thee, O God! We acknowledge thee to be the Lord!"

On another occasion, Mr. Wesley gives us this account:

After midnight, about a hundred of us walked home together, singing, rejoicing and praising God.

Often does this godly man make the record to this effect, "We continued in ministering the Word and in prayer and praise till morning."

One of his all-night wrestlings in prayer alone with God is said to have greatly affected a Catholic priest, who was really awakened by the occurrence to a realization of his spiritual condition.

As often as God manifested his power in scriptural times in working wonders through prayer, he has not left himself without witness in modern times. Prayer brings the Holy Spirit upon men today in answer to importunate, continued prayer just as it did before Pentecost. The wonders of prayer have not ceased.

15

Prayer and Divine Providence

PRAYER and the divine providence are closely related. They stand in close companionship. They cannot possibly be separated. So closely connected are they that to deny one is to abolish the other. Prayer supposes a providence, while providence is the result of and belongs to prayer. All answers to prayer are but the intervention of the providence of God in the affairs of men. Providence has to do specially with praying people. Prayer, providence, and the Holy Spirit are a trinity, which cooperate with each other and are in perfect harmony with one another. Prayer is but the request of man for God through the Holy Spirit to interfere in behalf of him who prays.

What is termed providence is the divine superintendence over earth and its affairs. It implies gracious provisions which Almighty God makes for all his creatures, animate and inanimate, intelligent or otherwise. Once we admit that God is the creator and preserver of all men, and concede that he is wise and intelligent, we are logically driven to the conclusion that Almighty God has a direct superintendence of those whom he has created and whom he preserves in being. In fact, creation and preservation suppose a superintending providence. What is called divine providence is simply Almighty God governing the world for its best interests, and overseeing everything for the good of mankind.

Men talk about a "general providence" as separate from a "special providence." There is no general providence but what is made up of special providences. A general supervision on the part of God supposes a special and individual supervision of each person, yes, even every creature, animal and all alike.

God is everywhere, watching, superintending, overseeing, governing everything in the highest interest of man, and carrying forward his plans and executing his purposes in creation and redemption. He is not an absentee God. He did not make the world with all that is in it, and turn it over to socalled natural laws, and then retire into the secret places of the universe having no regard for it or for the working of his laws. His hand is on the throttle. The work is not beyond his control. Earth's inhabitants and its affairs are not running independently of Almighty God.

Any and all providences are special providences, and prayer and this sort of providences work hand in hand. God's hand is in everything. None are beyond him nor beneath his notice. Not that God orders everything which comes to pass. Man is still a free agent, but the wisdom of Almighty God comes out when we remember that while man is free, and the devil is abroad in the land, God can superintend and overrule earth's affairs for the good of man and for his glory, and cause even the wrath of man to praise him.

Nothing occurs by accident under the superintendence of an all-wise and perfectly just God. Nothing happens by chance in God's moral or natural government. God is a God of order, a God of law, but nonetheless a superintendent in the interest of his intelligent and redeemed creatures. Nothing can take place without the knowledge of God.

> His all surrounding sight surveys
> Our rising and our rest;
> Our public walks, our private ways,
> The secrets of our breasts.

Jesus Christ sets this matter at rest when he says, "Are not two sparrows sold for a farthing? and one of them shall not fall on the ground without your Father. But the very hairs of your head are all numbered. Fear ye not, therefore, ye are of more value than many sparrows."

God cannot be ruled out of the world. The doctrine of prayer brings him directly into the world, and moves him to a direct interference with all of this world's affairs.

To rule Almighty God out of the providences of life is to strike a direct blow at prayer and its power. Nothing takes place in the world without God's consent, yet not in a sense that he either approves everything or is responsible for all things which happen. God is not the author of sin.

The question is sometimes asked, "Is God in everything?" as if there are some things which are outside of the government of God, beyond his attention, with which he is not concerned. If God is not in everything, what .is the Christian doing praying according to Paul's directions to the Philippians?

Be careful for nothing, but in everything, by prayer and supplication, with thanksgiving, let your requests be made known unto God.

Are we to pray for some things and about things with which God has nothing to do? According to the doctrine that God is not in everything, then we are outside the realm of God when "in everything we make our requests unto God.

Then what will we do with that large promise so comforting to all of God's saints in all ages and in all climes, a promise which belongs to prayer and which is embraced in a special providence: "And we know that all things work together for good to them that love God"?

If God is not in everything, then what are the things we are to expect from the "all things" which "work together for good to them that love God"? And if God is not in everything, in his providence what are the things which are to be left out of our praying? We can lay it down as a proposition, borne out by Scripture, which has a sure foundation, that nothing ever comes into the life of God's saints without his consent. God is always there when it occurs. He is not far away. He whose eye is on the sparrow is also upon his saints. His presence which fills immensity is always where his saints are. "Certainly I will be with thee," is the word of God to every child of his.

"The angel of the Lord encampeth round about them that fear him and delivereth them." And without God's permission, nothing can touch those who fear God. Nothing can break through the encampment without the permission of the captain of the Lord's hosts. Sorrows, afflictions, want, trouble, or even death, cannot enter this divine encampment without the consent of Almighty God, and even then it is to be used by God in his plans for the good of his saints and for carrying out his plans and purposes:

For I am persuaded that neither death, nor life, nor angels, nor principalities, nor powers, nor things present, nor things to come, Nor height, nor depth, nor any other creature, shall be able to separate us from the love of God which is in Christ Jesus our Lord.

These evil things, unpleasant and afflictive, may come with divine permission, but God is on the spot, his hand is in all of them, and he sees to it that they are woven into his plans. He causes them to be overruled for the good of his people, and eternal good is brought out of them. These things, with hundreds of others, belong to the disciplinary processes of Almighty God in administering his government for the children of men.

The providence of God reaches as far as the realm of prayer. It has to do with everything for which we pray. Nothing is too small for the eye of God, nothing too insignificant for his notice and his care. God's providence has to do with even the stumbling of the feet of his saints:

For he shall give his angels charge concerning thee, to keep thee in all thy ways. They shall bear thee up in their hands, lest thou dash thy foot against a stone.

Read again our Lord's words about the sparrow, for he says, "Five sparrows are sold for two farthings, and not one of them is forgotten before God." Paul asks the pointed question, "Doth God care for oxen?" His care reaches to the smallest things and has to do with the most insignificant matters which concern men. He who believes in the God of providence is prepared to see his hand in all things which come to him, and can pray over everything.

Not that the saint who trusts the God of providence, and who takes all things to God in prayer, can explain the mysteries of divine providence, but the praying ones recognize God in everything, see him in all that comes to them, and are ready to say as John said to Peter at the Sea of Galilee, "It is the Lord."

Praying saints do not presume to interpret God's dealings with them nor undertake to explain God's providences, but they have learned to trust God in the dark as well as in the light, to have faith in God even when "cares like a wild deluge come, and storms of sorrow fall."

"Though he slay me, yet will I trust him." Praying saints rest themselves on the words of Jesus to Peter, "What I do thou knowest not now but thou shalt know hereafter." None but the praying ones can see God's hands in the providences of life. "Blessed are the pure in heart, for they shall see God," shall see God here in his providences, in his Word, in his church. These are they who do not rule God out of earth's affairs, and who believe God interferes with matters of earth for them.

While God's providence is over all men, yet his supervision and administration of his government are peculiarly in the interest of his people.

Prayer brings God's providence into action. Prayer puts God to work in overseeing and directing earth's affairs for the good of men. Prayer opens the way when it is shut up or straitened.

Providence deals more especially with temporalities. It is in this realm that the providence of God shines brightest and is most apparent. It has to do with food and raiment, with business difficulties, with strangely interposing and saving from danger, and with helping in emergencies at very opportune and critical times.

The feeding of the Israelites during the wilderness journey is a striking illustration of the providence of God in taking care of the temporal wants of his people. His dealings with those people show how he provided for them in that long pilgrimage.

> Day by day the manna fell,
> O to learn this lesson well!
> Still by constant mercy fed,
> Give me, Lord, my daily bread.
> Day by day the promise reads,
> Daily strength for daily needs;
> Cast foreboding fears away,
> Take the manna of today.

Our Lord teaches this same lesson of a providence which clothes and feeds his people in the Sermon on the Mount when he says, "Take no thought what ye shall eat, or what ye shall drink, nor yet for your body, what ye shall put on." Then he directs attention to the fact that it is God's providence which feeds the fowls of the air, clothes the lilies of the field, and asks if God does all this for birds and flowers, will he not care for them?

All of this teaching leads up to the need of a childlike, implicit trust in an overruling providence, which looks after the temporal wants of the children of men. And let it be noted specially that all this teaching stands closely connected in the utterances of our Lord with what he says about prayer, thus closely connecting a divine oversight with prayer and its promises.

We have an impressive lesson on divine providence in the case of Elijah when he was sent to the brook Cherith, where God actually employed the ravens to feed his prophet. Here was an interposition so plain that God cannot be ruled out of life's temporalities. Before God will allow his servant to want bread, he moves the birds of the air to do his bidding and take care of his prophet.

Nor was this all. When the brook ran dry, God sent him to a poor widow, who had just enough meal and oil for the urgent needs of the good woman and her son. Yet she divided with him her last morsel of bread. What was the result? The providence of God interposed, and as long as the drought lasted, the cruse of oil never failed nor did the meal in the barrel give out.

The Old Testament sparkles with illustrations of the provisions of Almighty God for his people, and shows clearly God's overruling providence. In fact the Old Testament is largely the account of a providence which dealt with a peculiar people, anticipating their every temporal want, which ministered to them in emergencies, and which sanctified to them their troubles.

It is worthwhile to read that old hymn of Newton's, which has in it so much of the providence of God:

> Though troubles assail, and dangers affright,
> Though friends should all fail, and foes all unite,
> Yet one thing secures me, whatever betide,
> The promise assures us, the Lord will provide.
> The birds without barns, or storehouse are fed,
> From them let us learn, to trust for our bread;
> His saints what is fitting, shall ne'er be denied,
> So long as it's written, the Lord will provide.

In fact, many of our old hymns are filled with sentiments in song about a divine providence, which are worthwhile to be read and sung even in this day.

God is in the most afflictive and sorrowing events of life. All such events are subjects of prayer, and this is so for the reason that everything which comes into the life of the praying one is in the providence of God, and takes place under his superintending hand. Some would rule God out of the sad and hard things of life. They tell us that God has nothing to do with certain events which bring such grief to us. They say that God is not in the death of children, that they die from natural causes, and that it is but the working of natural laws.

Let us ask what are nature's laws but the laws of God, the laws by which God rules the world? And what is nature anyway? And who made nature? How great is the need to know that God is above nature, is in control of nature, and is in nature! We need to know that nature or natural laws are but the servants of Almighty God who made these laws, and that he is directly in them, and they are but the divine servants to carry out God's gracious designs, and are made to execute his gracious purposes. The God of providence, the God to whom the Christians pray, and the God who interposes in behalf of the children of men for their good, is above nature, in perfect and absolute control of all that belongs to nature. And no law of nature can crush the life out of even a child without God giving his consent, without such a sad event occurring directly under his all-seeing eye, and without his being immediately present.

David believed this doctrine when he fasted and prayed for the life of his child, for why pray and fast for a baby to be spared, if God has nothing to do with its death should it die?

Moreover, "does God care for oxen," and have a direct oversight of the sparrows which fall to the ground, and yet have nothing to do with the going out of this world of an immortal child? Still further, the death of a child, no matter if it should come alone as some people claim by the operation of the laws of nature, let it be kept in mind that it is a great affliction to the parents of the child. Where do these parents come in under any such doctrine? It becomes a great sorrow to mother and father. Are they not to recognize the hand of God in the death of the child? And to them is there no providence or divine oversight in the taking away of their child? David recognized the facts clearly that God had to do with keeping his child in life; that prayer might avail in saving his child from death, and that when the child died it was because God had ordered it. Prayer and providence in all this affair worked in harmonious cooperation, and David thoroughly understood it. No child ever dies without the direct permission of Almighty God, and such an event takes place in his providence for wise and beneficent ends. God works it into his plans concerning the child himself and the parents and all concerned. Moreover, it is a subject of prayer whether the child lives or dies.

> In each event of life how clear,
> Thy ruling hand I see;
> Each blessing to my soul most dear,
> Because conferred by thee.

16

Prayer and Divine Providence (Continued)

Two kinds of providences are seen in God's dealings with men, direct providences and permissive providences. God orders some things, others he permits. But when he permits an afflictive dispensation to come into the life of I' his saint, even though it originates in a wicked mind, and it is the act of a sinner, yet before it strikes his saint and touches him, it becomes God's providence to the saint. In other words, God consents to some things in this world many of them very painful and afflictive, without in the least being responsible for them, or in the least excusing him who originates them, but such events or things always become to the saint of God the providence of God to, him. So the saint can say in each and all of these sad and distressing experiences, "It is the Lord; let him do what seemeth him good." Or with the psalmist, he may say, "I was dumb; I opened not my mouth, because thou didst it."

This was the explanation of all of job's severe afflictions. They came to him in the providence of God, even though they had their origin in the mind of Satan, who devised them and put them into execution. God gave Satan permission to afflict job, to take away his property, and to rob him of his children. But job did not attribute these things to blind chance, nor to accident, neither did he charge them to satanic agency, but said, "The Lord hath given, and the Lord hath taken away;

blessed be the name of the Lord." He took these things as coming from his God, whom he feared and served and trusted.

And to the same effect are job's words to his wife when she left God out of the question, and wickedly told her husband, "Curse God and die." Job replied, "Thou speakest as one of the foolish women speaketh. What! Shall we receive good at the hand of God, and shall we not receive evil?"

It is no surprise under such a view of God's dealings with job that it should be recorded of this man of faith, "In all this did not job sin with his lips," and in another place was it said, "In all this job sinned not, nor charged God foolishly." In nothing concerning God and the events of life do men talk more foolishly and even wickedly than in ignorantly making up their judgments on the providences of God in this world. 0 that we had men after the type of job, who though afflictions and privations are severe in the extreme, yet they see the hand of God in providence and openly recognize God in it.

The sequel to all these painful experiences are but illustrations of that familiar text of Paul, "And we know that all things work together for good to them that love God." Job received back more in the end than was ever taken away from him. He emerged from under these tremendous troubles with victory, and became till this day the exponent and example of great patience and strong faith in God's providences. "Ye have heard of the patience of job," rings down the line of divine revelation. God took hold of the evil acts of Satan, and worked them into his plans and brgIIght great good out of them. He made evil work out for good without in the least endorsing the evil or conniving at it.

We have the same gracious truth of divine providence evidenced in the story of Joseph and his brethren, who sold him wickedly into Egypt and forsook him and deceived their old father. All this had its origin in their evil minds. And yet when it reached God's plans and purposes, it became God's providence both to Joseph and to the future of Jacob's descendants. Hear Joseph as he spoke to his brethren after he had revealed himself to them down in Egypt, as he traced all the painful events back to the mind of God and made them have to do with fulfilling God's purposes concerning Jacob and his posterity:

Now therefore be not grieved nor angry with yourselves that ye sold me hither; for God did send me before you to preserve life. And God sent me before you to preserve you a posterity on the earth, and to save your lives by a great deliverance. So that it was not you that sent me hither, but God.

Cowper's well-known hymn might well be read in this connection, one verse of which is sufficient just now:

God moves in a mysterious way, his wonders to perform;
He plants his footsteps in the sea, and rides upon the storm.

The very same line of argument appears in the betrayal of our Lord by Judas. Of course it was the wicked act of an evil man, but it never touched our Lord till the Father gave his consent, and God took the evil design of Judas and worked it into his own plans for the redemption of the world. It did not excuse Judas in the least that good came out of his wicked act, but it does magnify the wisdom and greatness of God in so overruling it that man's redemption was secured. It is so always in God's dealings with man. Things which come to us from second causes are no surprise to God, nor are they beyond his control. His hand can take hold of them in answer to prayer and he can make afflictions, from whatever quarter they may come, "work for us a far more exceeding and eternal weight of glory."

The providence of God goes before his saints, opens the way, removes difficulties, solves problems and brings deliverances when escape seems hopeless. God brought Israel out of Egypt by the hand of Moses, his chosen leader of that people. They came to the Red Sea. But there were the waters in front, with no crossing nor bridges. On one side were high mountains, and behind came the hosts of Pharaoh. Every avenue of escape was closed. There seemed no hope. Despair almost reigned. But there was one way open which men overlooked, and that was the upward way. A man of prayer, Moses, the man of faith in God, was on the ground. This man of prayer, who recognized God in providence, with commanding force, spoke to the people on this wise:

Fear ye not; stand still and see the salvation of the Lord.

With this he lifted up his rod, and according to divine command, he stretched his hand over the sea. The waters divided, and the command issued forth, "Speak unto the children of Israel that they go forward." And Israel went over the sea dry shod. God had opened a way, and what seemed an impossible emergency was remarkably turned into a wonderful deliverance. Nor is this the only time that God has interposed in behalf of his people when their way was shut up.

The whole history of the Jews is the story of God's providence. The Old Testament cannot be accepted as true without receiving the doctrine of a divine, overruling providence. The Bible is preeminently a divine revelation. It reveals things. It discovers, uncovers, brings to light things concerning God, his character, and his manner of governing this world, and its inhabitants, not discoverable by human reason, by science or by philosophy. The Bible is a book in which God reveals himself to men. And this is particularly true when we consider God's care of his creatures and his oversight of the world, his superintendent of its affairs. And to dispute the doctrine of providence is to discredit the entire revelation of God's Word. Everywhere this Word discovers God's hand in man's affairs.

The Old Testament especially, but also the New Testament, is the story of prayer and providence. It is the tale of God's dealings with men of prayer, men of faith in his direct interference in earth's affairs, and with God's manner of superintending the world in the interest of his people and in carrying forward his work in his plans and purposes in creation and redemption.

Praying men and God's providence go together. This was thoroughly understood by the praying ones of the Scripture. They prayed over everything because God had to do with everything. They took all things to God in prayer because they believed in a divine providence

THE POSSIBILITIES OF PRAYER

which had to do with all things. They believed in an everpresent God, who had not retired into the secret recesses of space, leaving his saints and his creatures to the mercy of a tyrant, called nature, and its laws, blind, unyielding, with no regard for anyone who stood in its way. If that be the correct conception of God, why pray to him? He is too far away to hear them when they pray, and too unconcerned to trouble himself about those on earth.

These men of prayer had an implicit faith in a God of special providence, who would gladly, promptly, and readily respond to their cries for help in times of need and in seasons of distress.

The so-called "laws of nature" did not trouble them in the least. God was above nature, in control of nature' while nature was but the servant of Almighty God. Nature's laws were but his own laws, since nature was but the offspring of the divine hand. Laws of nature might be suspended and no evil would result. Every intelligent person is conversant every day when he sees man overruling and overcoming the law of gravitation, and no one is surprised or raises his hand or voice in horror at the thought of nature's laws being violated. God is a God of law and order, and all his laws in nature, in providence and in grace work together in perfect accord, with no clash or disharmony.

God suspends or overcomes the laws of disease and rain often without or independent of prayer. But quite often he does this in answer to prayer. Prayer for rain or for dry weather is not outside the moral government of God, nor is it asking God to violate any law which he has made, but only asking him to give rain in his own way, according to his own laws. So also the prayer for the rebuking of disease is not a request at war with law either natural or otherwise, but is a prayer in accordance with law, even the law of prayer, a law set in operation by Almighty God as the so-called natural law which governs rain or which controls disease.

The believer in the law of prayer has strong ground on which to base his plea. And the believer in a divine providence, the companion of prayer, stands equally on strong granite foundations, from which he need not be shaken. These twin doctrines stand fast and will abide forever.

> In every condition, in sickness, in health,
> In poverty's vale or abounding in wealth;
> At home or abroad, on the land or the sea,
> As thy days may demand shall thy strength ever be.

APPENDIX: E. M. BOUNDS AND THE BOOKS HE WROTE

Edward McKenzie Bounds, also known as EM Bounds, is a name that may not be familiar to many people, but to Christians, he is a man who left an indelible mark in the field of prayer and spiritual revival. Born on August 15, 1835, in Shelby County, Missouri, Bounds was a Methodist minister and prolific writer whose books on prayer and fasting have impacted the lives of many Christians around the world.

Through his deep understanding of the power of prayer, Bounds sought to awaken Christians to the importance of prayer in their spiritual lives and draw them to a life of dependence on God.

Edward's father, Nehemiah, was a Circuit Riding Methodist preacher. Although Edward himself had a deep interest in spiritual matters from a young age, he did not enter the ministry until his late 30s. Once he did, his passion for prayer was evident, and he became a man who was known for his ministry of the Word and prayer.

Seeing prayer as the most essential duty of every Christian, Bounds and made it his life's work to encourage others to a life of prayer and intercession. He wrote several books on prayer that are still read and cherished by Christians worldwide. One of his most famous books, 'The Necessity of Prayer,' highlights the importance of prayer in the life of a believer.

The impact of EM Bounds' life and ministry is still felt today. His books have been translated into many languages and are still read and studied by millions of Christians worldwide. Bounds' teachings on prayer have been instrumental in the lives of many Christians who have experienced revival and the transformative power of prayer. His emphasis on the importance of a deep and meaningful prayer life has inspired many to seek a closer relationship with God through prayer and intercession.

Although he passed away over a century ago, Bounds' contribution to Christian literature has been recognized by many. Today, he is still considered to be a pioneer in the field of prayer and spiritual awakening. Books by E.M. Bounds include:

The Weapon of Prayer: An exploration of the power of prayer and how it can be used to overcome spiritual warfare. It offers practical guidance on how to use prayer as a powerful weapon against evil forces.

Power Through Prayer: Provides insights into the power of prayer and encourages readers to pray with faith and confidence. He explains how to use prayer as a tool for spiritual growth and transformation.

The Necessity of Prayer: Examines the importance of prayer in our lives and explains why it is necessary for us to have an intimate relationship with God through prayer. He also offers advice on how we can make our prayers more effective.

The Possibilities of Prayer: Explores the possibilities that come from praying faithfully and consistently. He encourages readers to develop their own personal style of prayer and shows them how they can use prayer as a means of deepening their relationship with God.

The Reality of Prayer: Looks at the reality behind prayer and what it means for our lives when we pray faithfully and consistently. He also explains why it is important to remember that God answers all prayers in His own way and time frame.

The Essentials Of Prayer: Talks about the essential elements that make up effective prayers, such as humility, faith, surrender, perseverance, obedience, trustworthiness, patience, courage, love and joyfulness. He also provides practical advice on how to make your prayers more meaningful and powerful.

Praying To Change Your Life: Examines how we can use prayer to transform our lives for the better by changing our attitudes towards ourselves and others around us. He emphasizes the importance of having a positive outlook on life in order to receive blessings from God through prayerful meditation and contemplation..

Purpose in Prayer: Focuses on understanding the purpose behind praying and why it is so important for us to do so daily in order to experience true peace within ourselves as well as with those around us..

Heaven's Cure for Earth's Care: Discusses how praying can help us find healing from physical pain or emotional distress by connecting us with God's grace.

The Essential of Intercession: Looks at intercessory praying--praying on behalf of others--and its significance in helping people achieve spiritual growth by allowing them to reach out beyond themselves.

The Power of Prayer and Fasting: Examines fasting along with praying as two different but complementary practices that are both essential in achieving spiritual growth.

The Secret of Intercession: Explores how intercessory praying can help bring about change not only in individual lives but also in society at large by influencing public opinion or policy decisions.

Prayer And Praying Men: This work delves into the concept of "praying men"—those who have dedicated themselves fully to a life devoted solely to prayer—and their role in spreading Christianity throughout history.

Prevailing Prayer to Peace: Focuses on finding inner peace through prevailing (persistent) prayers which are sustained over long periods until answered by God.

www.ingramcontent.com/pod-product-compliance
Lightning Source LLC
Chambersburg PA
CBHW070118080526
44586CB00013B/1330